Cosmologies

also by P.K.Page

POEMS

SELECTED

& NEW

BY *P. K. Page*

Cosmologies

EDITED &

INTRODUCED

BY *Eric Ormsby*

DAVID R. GODINE
Publisher · Boston

First U.S. edition published in 2003 by
DAVID R. GODINE, Publisher
Post Office Box 450
Jaffrey, New Hampshire 03452
www.godine.com

Copyright © 2002 P.K. Page

Originally published in 2002 as *Planet Earth: Poems
Selected and New* by The Porcupine's Quill

LCCN 2003111691

ISBN 1-56792-225-2

First U.S. printing, 2003
Manufactured in the United States of America

For Théa

❧ Contents

❧ Seven

❧ Journey 199

✎ Foreword

It has become customary in Canada to describe P.K. Page as
'distinguished', but that epithet betrays her. P.K. Page is simply
too vivacious, too cunning, too elusive to be monumentalized. She
is in fact the supreme escape artist of our literature. Try to confine
her in a villanelle and she scampers off into free verse. Peg her as
a prose poet and she springs forth with a glosa. Categorize her as
a poet who writes fiction but then note that you find very little
'poet's prose' in her stories. Her characters are often incised with
acid and a cruelly keen burin. She is the shrewdest of observers
but at the same time she celebrates life, low and high, in all its
manifestations. The humble mole is 'a haberdasher's sample of
wet velvet/moving on fine feet'. The Traveller's Palm is a
'miraculously plaited tree'. One of the finest and most distinctive
Canadian poets, P.K. Page is no provincial. She is a citizen not
merely of the world, but of the earth.

   Page's gift has always been too protean, too mercurial, for the
coarse mesh of our categories. That profusion is much in evidence
in the poems gathered here. Though they range in time over
several decades, it is in fact difficult to tell which are early works,
which more recent; all have the hard-won sheen of genuine
accomplishment from first to last. In style her work ranges from
pure song, such as the lyric 'Emergence', to longer, more intricate
stanzaic poems; such as, for example, the new poem included here
entitled 'Poem Canzonic with Love for AMK'. She is a master of
portraiture, of an often heartbreaking precision and compassion,
as in 'Schizophrenic' or 'Outcasts':

> search out the early misfit, who at school,
> sickly for love and giddy with his sex
> found friendship like a door banged in his face,
> his world a wasteland and himself a fool

Compassionate, but never sentimental. Page is also a brilliant
graphic artist and her sharp eye rarely falters. She herself defines
her credo in the poem for A.M. Klein:

It is the writer's duty to describe
freely, exactly. Nothing less will do.
Just as the painter must, from two make three
or conjure light, build pigments layer on layer
to form an artifact, so I must probe
with measuring mind and eye …

The reader new to P.K. Page's poetry will find a world depicted in vivid pigments, whether the landscape be Canadian or Brazilian. She is often likened to Elizabeth Bishop, who also sojourned memorably in Brazil, but the resemblance has always struck me as rather superficial. Bishop was also a fine poet and painter but her aims were narrower than Page's and her accomplishments, in the end, more modest. Page has an exuberance almost wholly lacking in Bishop. (The reader interested in comparing the two poets should look at Page's poem 'Poor Bird' in which she uses a line by Bishop as a refrain which is also an act of homage.) Indeed, there is something daunting in Page's ambition which seems to be nothing less than to take in the entire earth in all its variety and abundance.

Page is also frequently described as a 'survivor', a survivor of the generation that produced A.M. Klein, F.R. Scott, and others among her poet-friends. But this description, which makes her sound haggard and weather-beaten, also misleads. Anyone fortunate enough to have heard her read her work in public is immediately struck by her passion and her sense of humour. There is something wonderfully triumphant in her demeanour and it sounds in her voice as she reads. At Concordia University in Montreal, where I heard her a few years ago, I sat at the back of the auditorium and yet, even there, I felt encompassed by her vital force and energy which reached out to touch all who were present.

In selecting from the two volumes of her poems I have been guided by that instinct of vitality which emanates from all her finest work. P.K. Page herself has generously given me her own suggestions for inclusion and I have often accepted these; but as often as not, I have gone my own way. I have wanted to illustrate the immense range of her themes and concerns and to display the poetic skill and mastery which she has always brought to bear. The choice has been hard because there is so much. In her wonderful poem 'Planet Earth', which P.K. Page chose as the original title for this new selection, she begins with the lovely lines about the earth:

> It has to be loved the way a laundress loves her linens,
> the way she moves her hands caressing the fine muslins ...

This is the way too, I would suggest, in which P.K. Page's poems should be read and savoured, with all the senses, with the tips of the fingers and the surfaces of the skin, with that utmost attentiveness earth itself demands from us.

Eric Ormsby

✹ Planet Earth

It has to be spread out, the skin of this planet,
has to be ironed, the sea in its whiteness;
and the hands keep on moving,
smoothing the holy surfaces.

   'In Praise of Ironing', PABLO NERUDA

It has to be loved the way a laundress loves her linens,
the way she moves her hands caressing the fine muslins
knowing their warp and woof,
like a lover coaxing, or a mother praising.
It has to be loved as if it were embroidered
with flowers and birds and two joined hearts upon it.
It has to be stretched and stroked.
It has to be celebrated.
O this great beloved world and all the creatures in it.
It has to be spread out, the skin of this planet.

The trees must be washed, and the grasses and mosses.
They have to be polished as if made of green brass.
The rivers and little streams with their hidden cresses
and pale-coloured pebbles
and their fool's gold
must be washed and starched or shined into brightness,
the sheets of lake water
smoothed with the hand
and the foam of the oceans pressed into neatness.
It has to be ironed, the sea in its whiteness

and pleated and goffered, the flower-blue sea
the protean, wine-dark, grey, green, sea
with its metres of satin and bolts of brocade.
And sky – such an O! overhead – night and day
must be burnished and rubbed
by hands that are loving
so the blue blazons forth
and the stars keep on shining
within and above
and the hands keep on moving.

It has to be made bright, the skin of this planet
till it shines in the sun like gold leaf.
Archangels then will attend to its metals
and polish the rods of its rain.
Seraphim will stop singing hosannas
to shower it with blessings and blisses and praises
and, newly in love,
we must draw it and paint it
our pencils and brushes and loving caresses
smoothing the holy surfaces.

One

❧ Deaf Mute in the Pear Tree

His clumsy body is a golden fruit
pendulous in the pear tree

Blunt fingers among the multitudinous buds

Adriatic blue the sky above and through
the forking twigs

Sun ruddying tree's trunk, his trunk
his massive head thick-nobbed with burnished curls
tight-clenched in bud

(Painting by Generalić. Primitive.)

I watch him prune with silent secateurs

Boots in the crotch of branches shift their weight
heavily as oxen in a stall

Hear small inarticulate mews from his locked mouth
a kitten in a box

Pear clippings fall
                    soundlessly on the ground
Spring finches sing
                    soundlessly in the leaves

A stone. A stone in ears and on his tongue

Through palm and fingertip he knows the tree's
quick springtime pulse

Smells in its sap the sweet incipient pears

Pale sunlight's choppy water glistens on
his mutely snipping blades

and flags and scraps of blue
above him make regatta of the day

But when he sees his wife's foreshortened shape
sudden and silent in the grass below
uptilt its face to him

then air is kisses, kisses

stone dissolves

his locked throat finds a little door

and through it feathered joy
flies screaming like a jay

❧ The Flower Bed

Circular –
at a guess, twelve feet across –
and filled with a forest of sunflowers.
Girasoles turned sunward, yellow-lashed
black eyes staring at the sailing Sun.
No prospect of a blink
no fall or shift,
the focus constant, eye to eye engaged
as human eye can lock with human eye
and find within its ever-widening core,
such vastnesses of space
one's whole self tumbles in.

I see it in a glass or through a port,
crystalline,
refracting, like a globe,
its edges bending, sides distorted,
shine
of a thick lens,
the peep-hole through a door in which I *saw*
a tiny man
but *see* a bed of flowers
as bright as if enamelled yellow and green,
shooting their eye-beams at their Lord the Sun,
like so much spider's silk stretched true and taut.

And my own yellow eye, black lashed, provides
triangulation. We enmesh
three worlds with our geometry.
I learn,
in timeless Time at their green leafy school,
such silks and stares
such near-invisible straight curving lines
curving like Space itself
which merge and cross at the Omega point
and double back
to make transparent, multifoliate
Flowers of the Upper Air.

❧ The Mole

The mole goes down the slow dark personal passage –
a haberdasher's sample of wet velvet moving
on fine feet through an earth that only
the gardener and the excavator know.

The mole is a specialist and truly
opens his own doors; digs as he needs them
his tubular alleyways; and all his hills
are mountains left behind him.

❧ The Understatement

I speak not in hyperbole,
I speak in true words muted to their undertone,
choosing a pebble where you would a stone,
projecting pebbles to immensity.

For where love is no word can be compounded
extravagant enough to frame the kiss
and so I use the under-emphasis,
the muted note, the less than purely rounded.

❧ Portrait

He has pruned the roses every year and the secateurs
still shine and slice like butter through the wood
of the old standards he feels akin to, yet
he is a broth of a boy, this executive,
and would imagine (did he imagine) the rose tree of his blood
is rich with incipient blooms that he would cut
for a lady, were he in the mood.

Grandchildren flower about his slippers and this love
which gently lifts his heart is a kind of litmus
with its pink-blue variance, and saucer-sized.
Do the older ones suspect if they were to move
off quietly out of sight he would not miss
them at once, or ever, and only be surprised
they were so grown already to cast the harness?

Yet he cannot see himself as anything but a man
vigorous, strong-coloured, one in whom
action and contemplation met in youth
and grew close and became one,
so that his total – for he conceives it as a sum –
is, though it's not his language, behemoth,
a considerable figure in whatever room.

But there are other moments when the moment is
wanting a little, thinned out, watery,
as if a leg were swinging at the hip –
an undefined emotional diastasis.
But is he not a fool to accept the subnormality
of these temperatures, a fool to stoop
to a part in this half-lit minor tragedy?

The standard roses disciplined, the slow seasons,
the altering moment – quivering, intense –
spring into cameo focus and through his small
aperture a microscopic vision
is caught in the gelid lens:
bright leaves and blossoms, static, bloom and fall
in continuing and changeless violence.

✗ For G.E.R.

Neither the trailing and lifting of the remembered hand through water
nor the paling or flushing of the remembered skin
is as permanent with pain as footsteps in wet mortar
or winter settling in.

For the thought of the living image evades the eye
as quicksilver clutched, or the empty colour of wind;
and the remembered voice is soft with sound as a cloud across the sky.

The quicksilver splits and beads and the beads are shaken;
The wind dies out in a rattle among the trees,
and the cloud is blown and even the sky forsaken.

But the remembered voice, the remembered skin, the hand,
is sunlight only, or loveliness defined
in a young rain over a sun-baked land
or a visionary mind.

❧ Images of Angels

Imagine them as they were first conceived:
part musical instrument and part daisy
in a white manshape.
Imagine a crowd on the Elysian grass
playing ring-around-a-rosy,
mute except for their singing,
their gold smiles
gold sickle moons in the white sky of their faces.
Sex, neither male nor female,
name and race, in each case, simply angel.

Who, because they are white and gold, has made them holy
but never to be loved or petted, never to be friended?

Not children, who imagine them more simply,
see them more coloured and a deal more cosy,
yet somehow mixed with the father, fearful and fully
realized when the vanishing bed
floats in the darkness,
when the shifting point of focus, that drifting star,
has settled in the head.

More easily, perhaps, the little notary
who, given one as a pet, could not
walk the sun-dazzled street
with so lamb-white a companion.
For him its loom-large skeleton —
one less articulated than his own —
would dog his days with doom
until, behind the lethal lock
used for his legal documents
he guiltily shut it up.
His terror then that it escape
and smiling call for him at work.
Less dreadful for his public shame,

worse for his private guilt
if in that metal vault
it should die mute
and in the hour that he picked it up
he found it limp and boneless as a flower.

Perhaps, more certainly perhaps, the financier.
What businessman would buy as he buys stock
as many could cluster on a pin?
Angels are dropping, angels going up.
He could not mouth such phrases and chagrin
would sugar round his lips as he said 'angel'.
For though he mocks their mention he cannot
tie their tinsel image to a tree
without the momentary lowering of his lids
for fear that they exist in worlds which he
uneasy, reconstructs from childhood's memory.

The archeologist with his tidy science,
had he stumbled upon one unawares,
found as he finds an arrowhead, an angel,
a – what of a thing –
primitive as a daisy
might with his ice-cold eye have assessed it coolly.
But how, despite his detailed observations,
could he face his learned society and explain?
'Gentlemen, it is thought that they are born
with harps and haloes
as the unicorn with its horn.
Study discloses them white and gold as daisies.'

Perhaps only a dog could accept them wholly,
be happy to follow at their heels
and bark and romp with them in the green fields.

Or, take the nudes of Lawrence and impose
asexuality upon them; those
could meet with ease these gilded albinos.

Or a child, not knowing they were angels, could
wander along an avenue hand in hand
with his new milk-white playmates,
take a step
and all the telephone wires would become taut
as the high strings of a harp
and space be merely the spaces between strings
and the world mute, except for a thin singing,
as if a sphere – big enough to be in it
and yet small
so that a glance through the lashes
would show it whole –
were fashioned very finely out of wire
and turning in a wind.

But say the angelic word
and *this* innocent
with his almost unicorn
would let it go
for even a child would know
that angels should be flying in the sky,
and, feeling implicated in a lie,
his flesh would grow
cold
and snow
would cover the warm and sunny avenue.

✺ Arras

Consider a new habit – classical,
and trees espaliered on the wall like candelabra.
How still upon that lawn our sandalled feet.

But a peacock rattling its rattan tail and screaming
has found a point of entry. Through whose eye
did it insinuate in furled disguise
to shake its jewels and silk upon that grass?

The peaches hang like lanterns. No one joins
those figures on the arras.
                              Who am I
or who am I become that walking here
I am observer, other, Gemini,
starred for a green garden of cinema?

I ask, what did they deal me in this pack?
The cards, all suits, are royal when I look.
My fingers slipping on a monarch's face
twitch and go slack.
I want a hand to clutch, a heart to crack.

No one is moving now, the stillness is
infinite. If I should make a break ...
take to my springy heels ...? But nothing moves.
The spinning world is stuck upon its poles,
the stillness points a bone at me. I fear
the future on this arras.
                              I confess:

It was my eye.
Voluptuous it came.
Its head the ferrule and its lovely tail
folded so sweetly; it was strangely slim
to fit the retina. And then it shook

and was a peacock – living patina,
eye-bright – maculate!
Does no one care?

I thought their hands might hold me if I spoke.
I dreamed the bite of fingers in my flesh,
their poke smashed by an image, but they stand
as if within a treacle, motionless,
folding slow eyes on nothing. While they stare
another line has trolled the encircling air,
another bird assumes its furled disguise.

ꕥ Black Bamboo

This black
bamboo
is brushwork

Stalk
slim as a pen
Not quite
as black as ink

and tufted
at each node
with lanceolate
upthrusting
foliage

green chartreuse
and lime

    *

Once
in New Guinea Highlands
boys as slim
and black
as this astonishing
bamboo

and naked but for leaves
that seemed to grow
spontaneously
from their torsos –
part of them –
green
vegetable genitals
green
pubic hair –

leaped from the roadside
where our jeep had passed
to rearrange the stones
its tires displaced

remake the pattern
of their thoroughfare

    *

It was their road
They made it

Broke the rock
to build the roadbed
broke the rock again
to make a border –
almost a mosaic –

folk art
functional
and accurate
where warring tribes
could without trespass
pass

Their line of life

A safe and neutral space

    *

Now
with this gift
of black bamboo
I am
half naked in the heat
of humid high New Guinea
driving through
its rank green landscape

rancid pig fat

skin

And as our progress
rough and lumbering
scumbles the roadbed
scatters stones
like chicks

young ebony warriors –
the road gang –
spring
from their ambush
in the crotons clad
only in G-strings
armed with digging sticks
to make their high way
beautiful again

❧ A Grain of Sand

To See a World in a Grain of Sand
And a Heaven in a Wild Flower,
Hold Infinity in the palm of your hand,
And Eternity in an hour.

    Only a fly with its compound eye
an ant, a beetle, a dragonfly
or a child on a beach on a summer day
with time to idle the hours away
in the tiniest grain of sand can see
a limitless world of mystery
with suns that circle and stars that shoot
and golden boughs bearing silver fruit.
Can see in a daisy in the grass
angels and archangels pass
unfolding wings of dazzling white
to set the darkening earth alight.
See outer space become so small
that the hand of a child could hold it all.
Know eons pass, an hour slip by
like a scudding cloud in a windy sky.
With a wink and a blink an age is done.
Old Father Time is a boy again.

To See a World in a Grain of Sand
And a Heaven in a Wild Flower,
Hold Infinity in the palm of your hand,
And Eternity in an hour.

✒ Melanie's Nite-Book

Note

I am not Melanie.
We do not know one another.
Yet her poems found among my papers paint
the underside of something I have known –
a parallel existence in a key
significantly lower.

They have their place
strike their own note, distort, darken
the belling
light.

Mother

She said I gave her her jewelled breasts
and he, my father, her jewelled pubis
In return, she gave me a diamond heart
a splinter of ice for either eye

In this family potlatch I want no part
I am giving her back her diamond heart

Sister

Sister little idiot one
whom I loved
and who loved me
like a plant perhaps
or bird
tamed by kindness
set apart
from another planet
where
other laws prevail
and who
barely entered
in this race

part of me
O part of me

Father

Father, O farther
in what heaven circlest thou?
Daily and dearly
ask I for thy succour

I see thee now
the red crease on thy brow
left where thy cap had rested
Crested ring
Buttons of brightest brass
High boots' high shine
dusty with pollen

from the flowering grass
of that unrolling upland
whose sweet air
was black and white
with magpies' flight
rank sweat of thy black horse

Father, O farther
forcest thou me to range
world-wide world over
searching evermore
obedient, house-trained
heel-trained, at thy call?

Who settest the world on fire
for others quenched
my smallest fire
uncoiled its acrid smoke
Whose flute thou lettest
others hear, whose drum ...
My silence only
golden in thine ear

Father, O father
tremblest thou with dread
of my grey gaze
the twin of thy grey gaze?
I small, large-eyed
crunched in a tiny space
awaiting thy benediction
thy hand upon my head

Father, O father
cravest thou my grace?
Cravest forgiveness
for thy just rebukes
as I still crave thy praise

striving for thy approval
to appear
beautiful in thine eyes
or talented?

Father, father
can we call a truce?
Our binary stardom cancel
you from me
set free after how long –
two lifetimes? three? –
by that one word
which severs as it heals

Let me your spokesman
and your axeman be

Brother

You wore the looks I longed for
almond eyes
black from our gypsy forebears
milky skin
The creamy manner of your expensive school
lay sleek upon you
I was thin
acned and angular
No 'pretty girl'

Dreamed you displayed me
like a football trophy
took me to stag rock sessions
hockey games
places where I could loose
my female trace
my faint unearthly scent
my moon-pale face
Your slim twin sister
beautiful as Euclid

For it was written
All the ordered atoms
in orderly heaven
had ordained it so
And we obeyed that order
like a team
of harnessed horses driven
by skilled compassionate hands
or like a pair
of eagles riding
transparent muscles of air

Wakened to your abuse
the pale grey mornings
broke day after day
littered my room
your inkblots
on my notebooks
my stamps missing
no honey in the comb

Invented heroes to protect
young men
with fatal wounds
or dark congenital scars
White-meat invisible princes
sapphire-eyed
crippled
tubercular
Incurable invalids
who found me sweet as myrrh

These my companions
as I rode the subway
or climbed the interminable
steps to school
my co-conspirators
who let me love them
whom I called 'brother'
all my sister years

Ancestors

The cavernous theatre filled with them,
going back
generation on generation,
dressed in the colours of power:
scarlet and purple and black,
plumed and surpliced and gowned.
Men with arrogant Roman faces,
women like thoroughbred horses
held in check.

These were the people for whom
I had lived in exemplary fashion,
had not let down,
for whom I'd refrained from evil,
borne pain with grace.
And now they were here – resurrected –
the damned demanding dead,
jamming a theatre like head-cheese,
smelling of mothballs and scent,
brilliantine, shoe polish, Brasso
and old brocade.

Row after row
and tier after tier they ranged,
crowded together like eels
in the orchestra pit,
squeezed in the quilted boxes
and blocking the aisles
while I, on the stage alone,
last of the line,
pinned by the nails of their eyes,
was expected to give an account.

But the gypsies came in the nick
and flung themselves about.
They stamped their naked feet
dark with the dust of Spain,
clattered their castanets,
rattled their tambourines,
brandished their flashing knives
and put the lot to rout.

The Child

I dreamed the child was dead
and folded in a box
like stockings or a dress.

I dreamed its toys and games
its brightly coloured clothes
were lying on the grass

and with them I was left
adult and dutiful
with ink instead of blood.

I could not bear the grief
accommodate the loss –
as if my heart had died.

On wakening I saw
the child beside my bed
Not dead! not dead! I cried.

But startled by my voice
and fearful of my glance
the phantom infant fled.

Message

Not enough food

No drop of milk
No crumb

Only canned tongue

The Trail of Bread

What little the birds had overlooked
I found –
a first few meagre crumbs that led me on
from dark to darkest,
then the trail grew clear,
for deep in the airless wood
not even birds
ventured,
not enough sun,
no space to spread
their impeccable feathered arms.
(My wings were plucked.
Pin-feathers here and there.)

Whatever small rodents overlooked
I ate.
A skimpy nourishment.
It hurt my eyes
this meticulous search for food.
I might have stopped –
'stoppered', the word I want,
comparative,
a bottle sealed
inert, inanimate,
unable to move or open of itself.
(*I* could not move.
It moved me, opened me.)

Whatever they dropped for me
was miraculous,
multiple-purpose – food and way in one,
wakening me from nightmare,
leading on
out of that shadowy landscape
into dawn.

Rose of the air unfolding,
petal and thorn.
(A pencil sketch
with pale transparent wash –
watercolour on rice paper,
a wide brush.)
And sun, up with a rush.

The world gold-leafed and burnished:
gilded trees,
leaves like a jeweller's handwork,
grasses, ferns
filigreed and enamelled – Byzantine.
Cresses in clusters, bunched
beside a stream –
a glittering gold chain,
gold mesh, gold sheen,
where I bent down to drink.
(What birds then sang?)
Gold water in my mouth,
gold of my dreams
slipping like sovereigns
through my gold-rinsed hands.

Two

✒ Evening Dance of the Grey Flies

Grey flies, fragile, slender-winged and slender-legged
scribble a pencilled script across the sunlit lawn.

As grass and leaves grow black
the grey flies gleam –
their cursive flight a gold calligraphy.

It is the light that gilds their frail
bodies, makes them fat and bright as bees –
reflected or refracted light –

as once my fist
burnished by some beam I could not see
glowed like gold mail and conjured Charlemagne

as once your face
grey with illness and with age –
a silverpoint against the pillow's white –

shone suddenly like the sun
before you died.

✲ The Crow

By the wave rising, by the wave breaking
high to low;
by the wave riding the air, sweeping the high air low
in a white foam, in a suds,
there
like a churchwarden, like a stiff
turn-the-eye-inward old man
in a cutaway, in the mist
stands
the crow.

❧ The Hidden Room

I have been coming here since I was born
never at my will
only when it permits me

Like the Bodleian like the Web
like Borges' aleph
it embodies all

It is in a house
deeply hidden in my head
It is mine and notmine

yet if I seek it
it recedes
down corridors of ether

Each single version
is like and unlike
all the others

a hidden place
in cellar or attic
matrix of evil and good

a room
disguised as a non-room
a secret space

I am showing it to you
fearful you may not
guess its importance

that you will see only
a lumber room
a child's bolt-hole

Will not know it as prism
a magic square
the number nine

☙ Personal Landscape

Where the bog ends, there, where the ground lips, lovely
is love, not lonely.
                        Land is
love, round with it, where the hand is;
wide with love, cleared scrubland, grain
on a coin.
Oh, the wheatfield, the rock-bound rubble;
the untouched hills
                        as a thigh smooth;
the meadow.
Not only the poor soil lovely, the outworn prairie,
but the green upspringing,
the lark-land,
the promontory.

A lung-born land,
a breath spilling,
scanned by the valvular heart's
field glasses.

❧ About Death

1.

And at the moment of death
what is correct procedure?

Cut the umbilical, they said.

And with the umbilical cut
how then prepare the body?

Wash it in sacred water.
Dress it in silk for the wedding.

2.

I wash and iron for you
your final clothes
(my heart on your sleeve)
wishing to wash your flesh
wishing to close
your sightless eyes

nothing remains to do

I am a vacant house

❧ Custodian

I watch it.
Lock and stock.
No joke.
It is my job.

I dust, I wash, I guard
this fading fibre;
polish even.
Spit.

And rub I it
and shine
and wear it to the bone.
Lay bare its nub.

It is but matter
and it matters not
one whit or tittle
if I wear it out.

Yet mend I it and darn
and patch
and pat it even
like a dog

that which the Auctioneer
when I am gone,
for nearly nought
will knock down
from his block.

ℵ Finches Feeding

They fall like feathered cones from the tree above,
sumi the painted grass where the birdseed is,
skirl like a boiling pot
or a shallow within a river –
a bar of gravel breaking the water up.

Having said that, what have I said?
Not much.

Neither my delight nor the length of my watching is conveyed
and nothing profound recorded, yet these birds
as I observe them
stir such feelings up –
such yearnings for weightlessness, for hollow bones,
rapider heartbeat, east/west eyes
and such wonder – seemingly half remembered – as they rise
spontaneously into air, like feathered cones.

❧ Traveller's Palm

Miraculously plaited tree.
A sailor's knot
rooted,
a growing fan
whose grooved and slanted branches
are aqueducts
end-stopped
for tropical rains.

Knot, fan,
Quixote's windmill,
what-you-will –
for me, traveller,
a well.

On a hot day I took
a sharp and pointed knife,
plunged,
and water gushed
to my cupped mouth

old water
tasting green,
of vegetation and dust,
old water, warm as tears.

And in that tasting,
taster, water, air,
in temperature identical
were so
intricately merged
a fabulous foreign bird
flew silent from a void

lodged in my boughs.

⚡ Fly: On Webs

Two kinds of web: the one
not there. A sheet of glass.
Look! I am flying through air,
spinning in emptiness ... SPUNG!
... bounced on a flexible wire,
caught by invisible guys.

The other a filigree, gold
as the call of a trumpet. A sun
to my myriad-faceted eye.
A season. A climate. Compelled
and singing hosannas I fly:
I dazzle. I struggle. I drown.

❧ After Reading 'Albino Pheasants' by Patrick Lane

Pale beak … pale eye … the dark imagination
flares like magnesium. Add but *pale flesh*
and I am lifted to a weightless world:
watered cerulean, chrome yellow (light)
and green, veronese – if I remember – a soft wash
recalls a summer evening sky.

At Barra de Navidad we watched the sky
fade softly like a bruise. Was it imagination
that showed us Venus phosphorescent in a wash
of air and ozone? – a phosphorescence flesh
wears like a mantle in bright moonlight,
a natural skin-tone in that other world.

Why should I wish to escape this world?
Why should three phrases alter the colour of the sky
the clarity, texture even, of the light?
What is there about the irrepressible imagination
that the adjective *pale* modifying *beak, eye* and *flesh*
can set my sensibilities awash?

If with my thickest brush I were to lay a wash
of thinnest watercolour I could make a world
as unlike my own dense flesh
as the high-noon midsummer sky;
but it would not catch at my imagination
or change the waves or particles of light

yet *pale* can tip the scales, make light
this heavy planet. If I were to wash
everything I own in mercury, would imagination
run rampant in that suddenly silver world –
free me from gravity, set me floating sky-
ward – thistledown – permanently disburdened of my flesh?

Like cygnets hatched by ducks, our minds and flesh
are imprinted early – what to me is light
may be dark to one born under a sunny sky.
And however cool the water my truth won't wash
without shrinking except in its own world
which is one part matter, nine parts imagination.

I fear flesh which blocks imagination,
the light of reason which constricts the world.
Pale beak ... pale eye ... pale flesh ... My sky's awash.

✺ Chimney Fire

Something must be fire for them, these six
brass-helmeted navy-blue navvies come to chop
the old endlessly-polished wainscot with the fireman's axe.
Ready and royal for crisis and climax
shining and stalwart and valiant — for *this?*
Some element in this puny fire must prove
muscled enough for them to pit against,
and so they invade the green room, all six,
square up to its tidy silence and attack.

Only the roar in the brick and that abating
and the place orderly and quiet as a painting
of a house and all their paraphernalia outside waiting
to be used and useless and inside silence growing coolly
as a lily on a green stem.
Oh, how they tackle it, hack it, shout it down
only to find it broken out again,
implacably sending up suckers in the still room,
forevergreen, the chill obverse of flame.

Finally defeat it with their roaring laughter
and helmets on floor and armchair, drinking beer
like an advertisement for a brand name — 'after the fire
the dark blue conqueror relaxes here'
in an abandonment of blue and gold
that Rousseau the Douanier might have set
meticulously upon a canvas — those red brick
faces, vacant, those bright axes
and the weltering dark serge angles of arms and legs.

So they attacked their fire and put it out.
No tendril of silence grew in the green room when they went
into the night like night with only the six
stars of their helmets shining omnipotent
in a fiery constellation
pinking the darkness with a sign unknown
to ride the street like a flume, to fan to flame
smouldering branches of artery and vein
in beautiful conflagration, their lovely dream.

✹ Poor Bird

… looking for something, something, something.
Poor bird, he is obsessed!
The millions of grains are black, white, tan, and gray,
mixed with quartz grains, rose and amethyst.

  'Sandpiper', ELIZABETH BISHOP

From birth, from the first astonishing moment
when he pecked his way out of the shell, pure fluff,
he was looking for something – warmth, food, love
or light, or darkness – we are all the same stuff,
all have the same needs: to be one of the flock
or to stand apart, a singular fledgling.
So the search began – the endless search
that leads him onward – a vocation
year in, year out, morning to evening
looking for something, something, something.

Nothing will stop him. Although distracted
by nest-building, eggs, high winds, high tides
and too short a lifespan for him to plan
an intelligent search – still, on he goes
with his delicate legs and spillikin feet
and the wish to know what he's almost guessed.
Can't leave it alone, that stretch of sand.
Thinks himself Seurat (pointilliste)
or a molecular physicist.
Poor bird, he is obsessed!

And just because he has not yet found
what he doesn't know he is searching for
is not a sign he's off the track.
His track is the sedge, the sand, the suck
of the undertow, the line of shells.
Nor would he have it another way.
And yet – the nag – is there something else?
Something more, perhaps, or something less.
And though he examine them, day after day
the millions of grains are black, white, tan and gray.

But occasionally, when he least expects it,
in the glass of a wave a painted fish
like a work of art across his sight
reminds him of something he doesn't know
that he has been seeking his whole long life –
something that may not even exist!
Poor bird, indeed! Poor dazed creature!
Yet when his eye is sharp and sideways seeing
oh, *then* the quotidian unexceptional sand is
mixed with quartz grains, rose and amethyst.

✒ Cosmologies

I

Imagine eight universes – parallel.
The first is the one in which you said, 'I love you.'
I, weak with desire, wanted only your mouth.
In the others even the alphabet is different.

The first is the one in which you said, 'I love you.'
What, I ask, was heard in the other seven?
In the others even the alphabet is different
and we, cut off from higher frequencies.

What, I ask, was heard in the other seven?
The first is literal, material, flesh –
and we, cut off from higher frequencies,
blind inhabitants of a diving-bell.

The first is literal, material, flesh –
low C of an ascending scale.
Blind inhabitants of a diving-bell,
a leaf obliterates Mount Everest.

Low C of an ascending scale
as ordered as the colours of the rainbow.
A leaf obliterates Mount Everest.
Mouth, for me, the obliterating leaf.

As ordered as the colours of the rainbow,
the tonic sol-fa – its eight syllables.
Mouth for me, the obliterating leaf –
your mouth, saying the words, 'I love you.'

The tonic sol-fa – its eight syllables.
I, weak with desire, wanted only your mouth,
your mouth, saying the words, 'I love you.'
Imagine eight universes – parallel.

II

The second universe – is it like the first? –
grass, sky, blossoming trees in springtime,
rain, beloved waters, rivers, lakes,
during the dark months, rumour has it, snow.

Grass, sky, blossoming trees in springtime –
nature ostensibly the same as here.
During the dark months, rumour has it, snow
but temperate or not, we cannot know.

Nature ostensibly the same as here.
The colours slightly altered. The air softer.
But temperate or not, we cannot know
which is the prototype, and which the copy.

The colours slightly altered? The air softer?
Changes too subtle for our grosser senses.
Which is the prototype, and which the copy?
Paler or darker – how can we compare?

Changes too subtle for our grosser senses.
Geometry unreliable; and colours
paler or darker – how can we compare?
And do I love you less or love you more?

Geometry unreliable and colours.
Who are we in the second universe?
And do I love you less or love you more?
Our antic brains and fragile nervous systems.

Who are we in the second universe?
– Rain, beloved waters, rivers, lakes,
our antic brains and fragile nervous systems –
the second universe – is it like the first?

III

Now it is guesswork. Speculation fails.
The third is indecipherable, obscure.
Its stars, its solar systems, and its tao
are consummate, regardless of my view.

The third is indecipherable, obscure,
the fourth, the fifth, the entirety overhead
are consummate, regardless of my view.
My head is huge, an enlarged body part.

The fourth, the fifth, the entirety overhead
blow me away. I am a dandelion clock –
my head is huge, an enlarged body part,
free floating in an altered consciousness.

Blow me away, I am a dandelion clock
telling unreliable time at every breath
free floating in an altered consciousness –
in those not-to-be-imagined cosmoses.

Telling unreliable time at every breath
I become alpha, minus height and weight
in those not-to-be-imagined cosmoses.
Star-shine is far more wondrous than my light.

I become alpha. Minus height and weight.
Body amorphous – elbow, knee and ear.
Star-shine is far more wondrous than my light
in which I unknow all that I have known.

Body amorphous – elbow, knee and ear –
its stars, its solar systems and its tao
in which I unknow all that I have known.
Now it is guesswork. Speculation fails.

Three

✺ The Filled Pen

Eager to draw again,
find space in that small room
for my drawing-board and inks
and the huge revolving world
the delicate nib releases.

I have only to fill my pen
and the shifting gears begin:
flywheel and cogwheel start
their small-toothed interlock

and whatever machinery draws
is drawing through my fingers
and the shapes that I have drawn
gaze up into my eyes.
We stare each other down.

Light of late afternoon –
white wine across my paper –
the subject I would draw.
Light of the stars and sun.

Light of the swan-white moon.
The blazing light of trees.
And the rarely glimpsed bright face
behind the apparency of things.

❧ George Johnston Reading

A slow January, grey, the weather rainy.
Day after day after day the ceiling zero.
Then you arrive, comb honey from your hives pulled from
your suitcase, head full of metrics, syllable count,
rhyme – half-hidden, half rhyme and alliteration –
the poem's skeleton and ornamentation –
to give a reading as untheatrical as
it is subtle, elegant and unexpected.

I had not anticipated your translations
from Old Norse, your saga of heroic Gisli –
good man, strong man, man who could split an enemy
as butchers split a chicken, clean through the breastbone –
driven to running bloody, head drenched in redness,
dreamer of dark dreams prophetic of his downfall.
Writer of skaldic verses. Gisli, crow-feeder.
Great Gisli, dead of great wounds, son of whey-Thorbjorn.

Nor had I been prepared for those skaldic verse forms
(three-stressed lines in four pairs, final foot trochaic)
that made my head hum – their intricate small magic
working away like yeast till eight lines of court metre
are glittering and airy, furnished with pianos,
each short line, inexplicably a pianist
recreating for me the music of Scarlatti –
crossing hands on the keyboard, crossing and crossing.

Or – working away like bees in blossoms, shaking
a pollen of consonants on the audience
which sat, bundled and bunched in mufflers and greatcoats
in the bare unwelcoming hall where poets read
in Victoria, city of rainy winters.
And thinking about it now, I remember sun
and how honey sweetened the verses, made them gold
and tasting, that mid-January, of field-flowers.

❧ The Gold Sun

Trace the gold sun about the whitened sky
Without evasion by a single metaphor.
Look at it in its essential barrenness
And say this, this is the centre that I seek.

'Credences of Summer', WALLACE STEVENS

Sky whitened by a snow on which no swan
is visible, and no least feather falling
could possibly or impossibly be seen,
sky whitened like the blank page of a book,
no letters forming into words unless
written in paleness – a pallidity
faint as the little rising moons on nails –
and so, forgettable and so, forgot.
Blue eyes dark as lapis lazuli
trace the gold sun about the whitened sky.

You'll see the thing itself no matter what.
Though it may blind you, what else will suffice?
To smoke a glass or use a periscope
will give you other than the very thing,
or more, or elements too various.
So let the fabulous photographer
catch Phaeton in his lens and think he is
the thing itself, not knowing all the else
he is become. But you will see it clear
without evasion by a single metaphor.

How strip the sun of all comparisons?
That spinning coin – moving, yet at rest
in its outflinging course across the great
parabola of space – is Phoebus,
sovereign: heroic principle,
the heat and light of us. And gold – no less
a metaphor than sun – is not the least
less multiple and married. Therefore how
rid the gold sun of all its otherness?
Look at it in its essential barrenness.

Make a prime number of it, pure, and know
it indivisible and hold it so
in the white sky behind your lapis eyes.
Push aside everything that isn't sun
the way a sculptor works his stone,
the way a mystic masters the mystique
of making more by focusing on one
until at length, all images are gone
except the sun, the thing itself, deific,
and say this, this is the centre that I seek.

◗ Hologram

All that morning we looked at the citadel from every angle.
We began from the side in the shadow, where the sea,
Green without brilliance, – breast of a slain peacock,
Received us like time that has no break in it.

    'The King of Asine', GEORGE SEFERIS

It was astonishing, larger by far than we could imagine,
larger than sight itself but still we strained to see it.
It was Kafka's castle in a dream of wonder,
nightmare transmuted, black become golden,
buttresses disappearing in the cloud and azure:
a new geometry of interlocking octangles
and we, watching it, interlocked in a strange dimension –
that neither your heart nor mine could have invented –
of multiple images, complex as angels.
All that morning we looked at the citadel from every angle.

But that was later, after we had made the passage
from the faint light of morning star and pale moon
to unscrupulous noonday with its major chords –
battalions marching across an Escher landscape.
For us, at first, there was no hint of clarity,
no hint of anything that wasn't misty –
synaesthetic layers and lengths of space-time
leading us inward, downward, upward, as –
from all directions at once – observing closely,
we began from the side in the shadow and the sea.

Brave of us to begin in darkness. Or was it wisdom
that made us so prepare ourselves for that radiance
little by little? A Jurassic age must pass before even colour
could enter the scene – dawn's greys being so infinite
and infinitely subtle – transparencies, opacities.
And then we sensed it together – the tremulous foreshock
of what lay ahead: what could not be imagined,
possibly not even dreamed, a new range of experience.
And – unbelievably – what revealed itself as earthquake
was green, without brilliance, breast of a slain peacock.

But to the cones of our eyes that green was shining
and pierced us like a spear. (When joy is great enough
how distinguish it from pain?) And after the fugal greys
and the near-invisible shafts of no-colour that had stained us,
how could our eyes adjust to so full a spectrum?
And yet in a flash, from infra-red to ultraviolet,
we saw the hologram glittering above us
glistening in air we could suddenly enter like swallows
as the whole citadel, rainbowed, immediate,
received us like time that has no break in it.

✎ Dwelling Place

This habitation – bones and flesh and skin –
where I reside, proceeds through sun and rain
a mobile home with windows and a door
and pistons plunging, like a soft machine.

Conforming as a bus, its 'metal' is
more sensitive than chrome or brass. It knows
a pebble in its shoe or heat or cold.
I scrutinize it through some aperture

that gives me godsview – see it twist and change.
It sleeps, it weeps, its poor heart breaks,
it dances like a bear, it laughs, opines
(and therefore *is*). It has a leafy smell

of being young in all the halls of heaven.
It serves a term in anterooms of hell,
greying and losing lustre. It is dull.
A lifeless empty skin. I plot its course

and watch it as it moves – a house, a bus;
I, its inhabitant, indweller – eye
to that tiny chink where two worlds meet –
or – if you so discern it – two divide.

✒ Poem Canzonic with love to AMK

The sky is prussian blue, no, indigo
with just the merest hint of *ultramar*.
I am not painting it, so what care I?
And yet, I do care, deeply, as if life
depended on my skill to mix that blue.
Not my life only – your life, damn it! – <u>our</u>
whole planetary life:
the life of beetle, and ichneumon fly
plankton, crustacean, elk and polar bear
the delicate veined leaf
that blows against an enigmatic sky.

It is the writer's duty to describe
freely, exactly. Nothing less will do.
Just as the painter must, from two make three
or conjure light, build pigments layer on layer
to form an artefact, so I must probe
with measuring mind and eye to mix a blue
mainly composed of air.
What is my purpose? This I cannot say
unless, that I may somehow, anyhow
chronicle and compare
each least nuance and inconsistency.

This is the poem Abraham Moses Klein
wrote better, earlier, so why should I
write it again in this so difficult form?
His was a *tour de force*, a *cri de coeur*.
Mine is an urgent need to recombine
pigments and words, and so to rectify
and possibly restore
some lost arcanum from my past, some Om
secure, I thought, until I lost the key
or it lost me; before
birth intervened and – like a chloroform –

erased my archive, made me start again.
Vestigial memory only – vaguest dream
looming through mists, or like St. Elmo's fire
high in the riggings and phantasmal masts,
my one-eyed guide to seeing further in
or further out, to up-or-down the stream
of unremembered pasts –
might show me how to mix and how to name
that blue that is not cobalt or sapphire,
or fugitive, or fast;
and find the key that opens Here – and There.

❧ In Memoriam

The provinces of his body revolted,
The squares of his mind were empty,
Silence invaded the suburbs,
The current of his feeling failed: he became his admirers.

    'In Memory of W.B. Yeats', W.H. AUDEN

Rebel troops overran his palace.
A despot assumed the throne.
In his once peaceable kingdom
after the looting began
great bonfires eclipsed the moon.
The downtrodden all exulted
believing their time had come.
When his crown fell and his sceptre
and he was no longer consulted
the provinces of his body revolted.

In his perfectly tended parks
tall nettles sprang up and dockweed.
On his exhibition grounds
where merry-go-rounds had turned
and a Ferris wheel uptilted
the gypsies had broken camp.
Their rubbish alone was left.
He was a vacant lot,
he had become an exemption.
The squares of his mind were empty.

A light snow fell in summer.
His lakes were frozen over.
No forecaster had foreseen
such unseasonable weather.
Even his birds migrated.
Nothing could now disturb
the white infinity
of his radically altered syntax
the total absence of verbs.
Silence invaded the suburbs.

Only his nouns remained
and one by one they vanished.
Then when the traffic stopped
and silence invaded the towns
he became a soundless country.
We covered the many mirrors;
we covered his eyes with pennies.
His answering service broke down
and his state-of-the-art computers
the current of his feeling failed: he became his admirers.

❧ Address at Simon Fraser

Written in Victoria, B.C., during the unusually heavy snowfall of
February 1990, which brought to mind the even colder winter of 1989.

What do I have to tell you? I could wish
today was fifty years ago for then,
chock-full of schooling and high spirits, I
knew what was what. And where. And even when.
In other words, the word for it was on
the very tip of my too-talkative tongue.
Give me a subject – any subject – why
poetry and art could change the world,
and I could talk the stars out of the sky.
Not that I gave addresses, but with friends
I never lacked conviction.
               Now I know
a good deal less than fifty years ago.

So what am I to tell you? or to write?
I'm unconstrained. The space is adequate.
It's not a telegram I'm sending, nor
is paper rationed – yet. Although there may
be paper shortages before the day
is out, what with computers eating it.
               And the way
they cut the trees down – you might say
they thought them hay. But that ain't hay –
that is the planet's lungs.
               I hear you say,
'The subject is a bore, and anyway,
we've said it all before. What devastation!
we've said, seeing the clear-cut ravaged land.
Whose do they think the trees are anyway?
we've said. Cliché. Cliché. Cliché.'
But just whose are they? Think about it. Whose?
The planet may be watching this abuse.

To change the focus, winter's here. It's cold,
much colder than we're used to on this coast,
a fact that either proves or contradicts
the greenhouse theory, depending upon which
scientist you are reading. Outside, snow
from an Arctic movie blows and drifts.
We're bundled up in comforters and coats.
I'm cooking with my gloves on — what a gas! —
over the butane burner bought for just
such an eventuality as this.

Some of us have no water, some no power.
And some have floods: the frozen pipes have burst,
the broken waters freezing on the floor.
One friend says she could skate on the Tabriz
inherited from an aunt — a layer of ice
is glazing all the woven leaves and flowers,
and calls to mind the crystallized violets she
ate at that same aunt's dinner table once,
a small, enraptured child. What, eat a flower?

In nature, leaves and flowers are freezing too.
So overeager — some, already out,
are little sherbets on their frosted stems,
and some have lost their buds. How can I bear
to think the *ostara* hyacinths may be dead? —
their curling, crisp blue petals and their scent
of heaven filling all the sky-blue air ...

I hope they can survive it, if I can't.
Of course I can, but there are problems. One,
I cannot get the car out. If I could,
the street is glare ice and the nearest hill
is now a frozen, rutted, glassy chute
better for bobsleds than jalopies. So
I cool my heels at home, and wait it out.

I hear you say – (who are you, by the way,
so quick to interrupt me. Are you me
disguised, a kind of phantom limb,
equipped with larynx and a point of view?
or, to reverse the question, am I you?)

– I hear you say, provocatively, 'How
account for planetary warming now?
As no one knows for certain, let's suppose
the greenhouse boys are mad, or wrong or blind.
Then we can put their nonsense out of mind
till they are proven right.'
                    O Nero dear,
can you not stop your fiddling and hear
the flicker of those small flames drawing near?
Once it is proven, it will be too late.

Meanwhile, what should we do about it? should
'I part my hair behind?' or dedicate
my whole life, or my half life if you will,
to lobbying politicians? (What a fate!)
or making speeches which I rarely do?
Polemics. Mercy! I was never good
at argument or logic, never felt
the writer had a role beyond the role
of writing what he/she *must* write, but if
the whole great beautiful caboodle hangs
in the balance – (d'you remember how
celestial our planet looked from space
and how the astronauts who saw it small
floating above/below them like a ball
thrown to delight a child, returned to view
their world transformed – beauty is in the eye –
[Is hell then heaven if we see it so?]
and they, the astronauts, transformed as well) –

and, if our future here is unconfirmed,
and we are on probation, maybe I
must change my tune, my scale even, and try
some left-brain reasoned thinking, learn to write
well-argued dissertations and forget
poetry and the arts I love.
                    And yet
I can't believe it. Surely art is more
important than it ever was before –
Before! Before what? Curious how we wear
binary blinkers: BC and AD.
Even our global history can be *pre*
which shows we see it finite, as if we,
homo sapiens, had invented it.
(It all began with us – like love and sex!)
We are such one-eyed kings, or one-eyed jacks.
There are no one-eyed queens. Go check your packs.

Surely our break with nature is the source
of all that's out of kilter, out of sync.
How can a city dweller visualize
a world unpavemented, unstreetlamped? or
imagine how the constellations shine
as night ingathers earth and sets alight
the topaz pole star pulsing in the north –
front runner of vast galaxies that stretch
clustered in patterns like huge honeycombs.
The jury's out on this, and who am I,
neither astronomer nor scientist,
to venture an informed opinion? Yet
the mere idea of honeycombing space
so matches with some image in my head
that when I read the story in the press
I shouted 'snap', and saw, as in a flash,
the whole hexagonal geometry.

And how can youngsters who have never seen
a seed by slow degrees become a shoot,
conceptualize, except in their own loins,
'the force that through the green fuse drives the flower'?
A city boy I know won't eat a pear
picked from a green, unsanitary tree,
balks at the thought of it, prefers the bland
and un-sunripened, supermarket fruit
refrigerated, plastic-wrapped, germ-free.
Is he the symbol of an age that's lost
its evolutionary memory?

But to get back to art, for there my heart is,
there – beyond materiality,
beyond the buy-and-sell, beyond the want
embedded in us, and beyond desire –
resides the magic greed has cancelled out.
If we'll but give it time, a work of art
'can rap and knock and enter in our souls'
and re-align us – all our molecules –
to make us whole again. A work of art,
could, 'had we but world enough and time,'
portray for us – all Paradise apart–
'the face (we) had/before the world was made,'
or, to compound the image, vivify
Plato's invisible reality.

But is there time enough? This turning world
we call our home, or *notre pays* – could
become inimical to humankind –
humanunkind as cummings might have said –
in fewer years than I have walked this earth.

So, what is there to tell you? Only this.
'Imagination is the star in man.'
Read *woman*, if you wish. And though we are
trapped in the body of an animal,
we're half angelic, and our angel ear,
which hears the music of the spheres, can hear
the planet's message, dark, admonishing,
as the archaic torso of Apollo
admonished Rilke, 'You must change your life.'

Art and the planet tell us. Change your life.

Four

✺ Outcasts

Subjects of bawdy jokes and by the police
treated as criminals, these lovers dwell
deep in their steep albino love –
a tropic area where nothing grows.

Nobody's brothers, they revolve
on rims of the family circle, seek some place
where nothing shuns them, where no face
in greeting dons the starched immaculate mask.

Look, in their isolation they become
almost devoid of bones, their ward is one
nobody enters, but their least
window requires a curtain. They are clowns

without a private dressing room, with only
one ancient joke to crack now and forever.
They draw a crowd as if they had a band:
Always the healthy are their audiences.

The youths who hunt in packs, bitches with cash,
crafty embezzlers of the public purse,
perjurers and fashionable quacks
slumming, but saintly, saintly, judge them as

outcasts. In the laundered mind they rate
the bottom of the scale, below the Jew
with his hundred hands and pockets and below
niggers whose love is lewd.

Let doctors show a white aseptic hand
within their sickroom and let parents gaze
back against time's tight fist to find the cause –
seek in the child the answer to the man:

search out the early misfit, who at school,
sickly for love and giddy with his sex
found friendship like a door banged in his face,
his world a wasteland and himself a fool.

✸ Schizophrenic

Nobody knew when it would start again –
the extraordinary beast go violent in her blood;
nobody knew the virtue of her need
to shape her face to the giant in her brain.

Certainly friends were sympathetic, kind,
gave her small handkerchiefs and showed her tricks,
built her life to a sort of pick-up-sticks
simplification – as if she were a child.

Malleable she wore her lustre nails
daily like a debutante and smoked,
watching the fur her breath made as they joked,
caught like a wind in the freedom of their sails.

While always behind her face, the giant's face
struggled to break the matte mask of her skin –
and, turned about at last, be looking in –
tranquilly *in* to that imprisoned place.

Strong for the dive he dived one day at tea –
the cakes like flowers, the cups dreamy with cream –
he saw the window a lake and with a scream
nobody heard, shot by immediacy,

he forced the contours of her features out.
Her tea-time friends were statues as she passed,
pushed, but seemingly drawn towards the glass;

her tea-time friends were blind, they did not see
the violence of his struggle to get free,
and deaf, and deaf, they did not hear his shout.

The waters of his lake were sharp and cold –
splashed and broke, triangular on the floor
after the dive from his imagined shore
in a land where all the inhabitants are old.

❧ Man with One Small Hand

One hand is smaller than the other. It
must always be loved a little like a child;
requires attention constantly, implies
it needs his frequent glance to nurture it.

He holds it sometimes with the larger one
as adults lead a child across a street.
Finding it his and suddenly alien
rallies his interest and his sympathy.

Sometimes you come upon him unawares
just quietly staring at it where it lies
as mute and somehow perfect as a flower.

But no. It is not perfect. He admits
it has its faults: it is not strong or quick.
At night it vanishes to reappear
in dreams full-size, lost or surrealist.

Yet has its place like memory or a dog –
is never completely out of mind – a rod
to measure all uncertainties against.

Perhaps he loves it too much, sets too much stock
simply in its existence. Ah, but look!
It has its magic. See how it will fit
so sweetly, sweetly in the infant's glove.

✎ Another Space

Those people in a circle on the sand
are dark against its gold
turn like a wheel
revolving in a horizontal plane
whose axis – do I dream it? –
vertical
invisible
immeasurably tall
rotates a starry spool.

Yet *if* I dream
why in the name of heaven are fixed parts
within me set in motion
like a poem?

Those people in a circle reel me in.
Down the whole length of golden beach I come
willingly pulled by their rotation
slow
as a moon pulls waters
on a string
their turning circle winds around its rim.

I see them there in three dimensions yet
their height implies another space
their clothes'
surprising chiaroscuro postulates
a different spectrum.
What kaleidoscope
does air construct
that all their movements make a compass rose
surging and altering?
I speculate
on some dimension I can barely guess.

Nearer I see them dark-skinned.
They are dark. And beautiful.
Great human sunflowers spinning in a ring
cosmic as any bumble-top
the vast
procession of the planets in their dance.
And nearer still I see them – 'a Chagall' –
each fiddling on an instrument – its strings
of some black woollen fibre
and its bow – feathered –
an arrow almost.
                    Arrow *is*.

For now the headman – one step forward shoots
(or does he bow or does he lift a kite
up and over the bright pale dunes of air?)
to strike the absolute centre of my skull
my absolute centre somehow
with such skill
such staggering lightness
that the blow is love.

And something in me melts.
It is as if a glass partition melts –
or something I had always thought was glass –
some pane that halved my heart
is proved, in its melting, ice.

And to-fro all the atoms pass
in bright osmosis
hitherto
in stasis locked
where now a new
direction opens like an eye.

❧ Seraphim

In the dream it was the seraphim who came
golden, six-winged
with eyes of aquamarine
and set my hair aflame
and spoke in a language which written down –
an elegant script of candelabras and chalices –
spelled out my name

but it was not my name

The mornings following were bright as wings
sky's intricate cirrus
the feathers under his wings
the wind's great rush
the bladed beat of his wings

Mare's tails traced the passage of his seraphic chariot

Hummingbirds ruby-throated roared and braked
in the timeless isinglass air and burned like coals
high in the fronds of a brass palm sunbirds sang
girasoles swung their cadmium-coloured hair
and I heard the seraphim telling once again
the letters of my name

but my name was lost in the spoken syllables

✈ The Disguises

You, my Lord, were dressed in astonishing disguises:
as a Chinese emperor, ten feet tall,
as a milk-skinned woman
parading in exquisite stuffs.

You were ambiguous and secret
and hidden in other faces.

How did we know you were there at all?
Your ineffable presence
perfumed the air like an avenue of lilacs.

◊ Inebriate

During the day I laugh and during the night I sleep.
My favourite cooks prepare my meals,
my body cleans and repairs itself,
and all my work goes well.

> 'I Have Not Lingered in European Monasteries',
> LEONARD COHEN

Here is eternity as we dream it – perfect.
Another dimension. Here the ship of state
has sprung no leaks, the captain doesn't lie.
The days are perfect and each perfect minute
extends itself forever at my wish.
Unending sunlight falls upon the steep
slope of the hillside where the children play.
And I am beautiful. I know my worth
and when I smile I show my perfect teeth.
During the day I laugh and during the night I sleep.

A dreamless, healing sleep. I waken
to everlasting Greece as white and blue
as music in my head –
an innocent music.
I had forgotten such innocence exists,
forgotten how it feels
to live with neither calendars nor clocks.
I had forgotten how to un-me myself.
Now, as I practise how and my psyche heals,
my favourite cooks prepare my meals.

I am not without appetite, nor am I greedy.
My needs are as undemanding as my tastes:
spring water, olives, cucumber and figs
and a small fish on a white plate.
To lift my heart I have no wish for wine –
the sparkling air is my aperitif.
Like Emily I am inebriate.
Rude health is mine – and privilege. I bathe
in sacred waters of the river Alph.
My body cleans and repairs itself.

Poised between Earth and Heaven, here I stand
proportions perfect – arms and legs outspread
within a circle – Leonardo's man.
So do I see the giddy Cosmos. Stars
beyond stars unfold for me and shine.
My telephoto lens makes visible
time future and time past, and timeless time
receives me like its child. I am become
as intricate and simple as a cell
and all my work goes well.

⚘ Knitters

These women knitting knit a kind of mist –
climate of labyrinth –
into the air.
Sitting like sleepers,
propped against the chintz,
pin-headed somehow – figures by Moore –
arachnes in their webs, they barely stir –

except their eyes and hands, which wired to some
urgent personal circuit,
move as if
a switch controlled them.
Hear the click and hum
as their machines, translating hieroglyphs,
compulsive and monotonous, consume –
lozenge and hank – the candy-coloured stuff.

See two observe the ceremony of skeins:
one, forearms raised,
the loops around her palms,
cat's-cradle rocks, is metronome, becalmed;
while her companion
spun from her as from
a wooden spindle, winds a woollen world.

A man rings like an axe, is alien,
imperilled by them,
finds them cold and far.
They count their stitches on a female star
and speak another language,
are not kin.
Or is he Theseus remembering
that maze, those daedal ways; the Minotaur?

They knit him out, the wool grows thick and fills
the room they sit in like a fur
as vegetable more than animal,
surrealist and slightly sinister,
driven by motors strong beyond their wills,
these milky plants devour
more hanks of wool, more cubic feet of air.

✒ Bank Strike

Quebec, 1942

When the time came,
after the historied waiting,
they were ready with their strikers' jackets
and their painted signs 'En Grève',
facing the known streets
and the rough serge knees and elbows
of police.

Time was bald on their skins,
their desks and counters and cages
cried in their eyes like a strategical retreat
and the unrelieved picket line
had a stained, for-all-time permanence
on the distorted street.

In the foreground church
the flames of the sacred candles
burned, in their suddenly foreign homes
their meals were stiff as religious paintings
and the bullet of 'fired'
was wedged in their skulls.

Yet from the cellar of certainty they came
up the long escalator to defeat,
their hearts hurting their ribs, their hands heavy;
blew hot and cold
and scratched the solid curb
like weather worrying an iron city.

✳ The Permanent Tourists

Somnolent through landscapes and by trees
nondescript, almost anonymous,
they alter as they enter foreign cities –
the terrible tourists with their empty eyes
longing to be filled with monuments.

Verge upon statues in the public squares
remembering the promise of memorials
yet never enter the entire event
as dogs, abroad in any kind of weather,
move perfectly within their rainy climate.

Lock themselves into snapshots on the steps
of monolithic bronze as if suspecting
the subtle mourning of the photograph
might, later, conjure in the memory
all they are now incapable of feeling.

And track all heroes down: the boy who gave
his life to save a town; the stolid queen;
forgotten politicians minus names;
the plunging war dead, permanently brave,
forever and ever going down to death.

Look, you can see them nude in any café
reading their histories from the bill of fare,
creating futures from a foreign teacup.
Philosophies like ferns bloom from the fable
that travel is broadening at the café table.

Yet, somehow beautiful, they stamp the plaza.
Classic in their anxiety they call
all the memorials of naked stone
into their passive eyes, as placid rivers
are always calling to the ruined columns.

✈ The Inarticulate

Dumb are their tongues and doubtful their belief.
And grown too slow to speak,
grow double dumb,
misers of words and miserable when wrapped
tight in a sentence.
(O move the comma half an inch for head
to slip and wriggle through –
the final latch
clicks with the word of sense.)

I see them daily, inarticulate,
on streetcar and on street;
work at their desks
and worm my hearing underneath their skulls,
die from the silence rooted in their tongues,
slide like a cup upon their screaming eyes
and feel the sirens blowing in their necks
vibrate too high for sound.

They wither, tuned for sound, who cannot speak,
hammer all day at keys that do not print,
and file their voices in the teeming vault.
Learning the language of the deaf and dumb
their prayers are lit, but studying fingers creak.
Like foreign papers, no one reads their hands.

❧ Young Girls

Nothing, not even fear of punishment
can stop the giggle in a girl.
Oh, mothers' trim
shapes on the chesterfield cannot dispel
their lolloping fatness.
Adolescence tumbles about in them
on the cinder schoolyard or behind the expensive gates.

See them in class like porpoises
with smiles and tears
loosed from the same subterranean faucet; some
find individual adventure in
the obtuse angle, some in a phrase
that leaps like a smaller fish from a sea of words.
But most, deep in their daze, dawdle and roll;
their little breasts like wounds beneath their clothes.

A shoal of them in a room makes it a pool.
How can one teacher keep the water out,
or, being adult, find the springs and taps
of their tempers and tortures?
Who, on a field filled with their female cries
can reel them in on a line of words
or land them neatly in a net?
On the dry ground they goggle, flounder, flap.

Too much weeping in them and unfamiliar blood
has set them perilously afloat.
Not divers these – but as if the waters rose in flood
making them partially amphibious
and always drowning a little and hearing bells;
until the day the shoreline wavers less,
and caught and swung on the bright hooks of their sex,
earth becomes home – their natural element.

✷ Landlady

Through sepia air the boarders come and go
impersonal as trains. Pass silently
the craving silence swallowing her speech;
click doors like shutters on her camera eye.

Because of her their lives become exact:
their entrances and exits are designed;
phone calls are cryptic. Oh, her ticklish ears
advance and fall back stunned.

Nothing is unprepared. They hold the walls
about them when they weep or laugh. Each face
is dialled to zero publicly. She peers
stippled with curious flesh;

pads on the patient landing like a pulse,
unlocks their keyholes with the wire of sight,
searches their rooms for clues when they are out,
pricks when they come home late.

Wonders when they are quiet, jumps when they move,
dreams that they dope or drink, trembles to know
the traffic of their brains, jaywalks their street
in clumsy shoes.

Yet knows them better than their closest friends:
their cupboards and the secrets of their drawers,
their books, their private mail, their photographs
are theirs and hers.

Knows when they wash, how frequently their clothes
go to the cleaners, what they like to eat,
their curvature of health, but even so
is not content,

and, like a lover, must know all, all, all.
Prays she may catch them unprepared at last
and palm the dreadful riddle of their skulls –
hoping the worst.

✒ Element

Feeling my face has the terrible shine of fish
caught and swung on a line under the sun
I am frightened, held in the light that people make
and sink in darkness freed and whole again
as fish returned by dream into the stream.

Oh, running water is not rough: ruffled to eye,
to flesh it's flat and smooth; to fish
silken as children's hands in milk.

I am not wishful in this dream of immersion.
Mouth becomes full with darkness
and the shine, mottled and pastel, sounds its own note, not
the fake high treble thrown on resounding faces.

There are flowers – and this is pretty for the summer –
light on the bed of darkness; there are stones
that glisten and grow slime;
winters that question nothing, are a new
night for the passing movement of fine fins;
and quietly, by the reeds or the water fronds
something can cry without discovery.

Ah, in daylight the shine is single
as dime flipped or gull on fire or fish
silently hurt – its mouth alive with metal.

❧ The Sick

All these, the horizontal and inactive,
held in the fronds of fever
or crooks of pain,
with their many pupilled and respective
eyes floating like water flowers on a stagnant river
or tight and walled as stone,
inhabit a country that is all their own.

Lie on the personal white plains of beds
but not as sleepers do,
giving themselves,
nor yet as lovers, windmills in their heads;
but emptied out as hoof-prints where the cattle go,
they live, pathetic halves,
pallidly hoping to complete themselves.

Some in the levitation of half sleep
with heads like dandelions
seeded and soft
have lost their bodies as they lost their hopes
and float like freaks in air – pneumatic scions –
inflated by a cough
to altitudes where there is nothing left.

Others as white as nurses, clean as soap,
drift in a scent of pink
with roses nudging them
into a patent and elastic sleep
where they can soar with suns before they sink
below the nurses' hems
single and cool and fresh as roses' stems.

While all the others in the coal-hole dark,
lighting their own despair
and unattended
except by bills and fears about their work,
are pale as oysters when exposed to air
and illness ended,
the thing that's broken in them is not mended.

For loneliness and fear signal like scouts
in jumping semaphore
from head to heart,
or joined, light flares and never put them out
and from the dying ones, set fire to more;
so, single as a dart
the body is; as single as a dart

and yet is multiple, rubs shoulders with
twins at each corner
shakes its own hands
while meeting foreigners and living myths
and rarely knows itself to be the owner
of common dividends
through having interest in a hundred lands.

❧ Squatters

So orderly was their conduct it was as if
chessmen had suddenly moved of their own accord
under beneficent darkness across the stiff
squares of the board.

Tired of waiting for the hovering hands'
strategic gestures, for the minds' approved
consideration, they made their demands
and received the inadequate answers before they moved.

Entered the empty house without right of entry,
a phosphorescence issuing from their action,
feeling at last they entered their own country
from a new direction.

Were citizens and individuals once
they became a community; they understood
the clear simplicity of omnipotence
in planning from common need for a common good.

But they had committed the most outrageous act:
they were neither violent nor tough,
every action had been circumspect.
Obviously they could not be hated enough.

🐦 Only Child

The early conflict made him pale
and when he woke from those long weeping slumbers she was there
and the air about them – hers and his –
sometimes a comfort to him, like a quilt, but more
often than not a fear.

There were times he went away – he knew not where –
over the fields or scuffing to the shore,
suffered her eagerness on his return
for news of him – where had he been, what done?
He hardly knew and didn't wish to know
or think about it vocally or share
his private world with her.

Then they would plan another walk, a long
adventure in the country, for her sake –
in search of birds. Perhaps they'd find the blue
heron today, for sure the kittiwake.

Birds were familiar to him now, he knew
them by their feathers and a shyness like his own,
soft in the silence.
By the pool she said, 'Observe,
the canvasback's a diver,' and her words
stuccoed the slaty water of the lake.

He had no wish to separate them in groups
or learn the Latin,
or, waking early to their songs remark, 'The thrush,'
or say at evening when the air is streaked
with certain swerving flying,
'Ah, the swifts.'

Birds were his element like air and not
her words for them – making them statues
setting them apart,
nor were they lots of little facts and details like a book.
When she said, 'Look!'
he let his eyeballs harden
and when two came and nested in the garden
he felt their softness, gentle, near his heart.

She gave him pictures, which he avoided, showing
them flat and coloured on a painted land.
Rather would he lie in the grass, the deep grass of the island
close to the gulls' nests, knowing
these things he loved and needed by his hand,
untouched and hardly seen but deeply understood.
Or sail among them through a wet wind feeling
their wings within his blood.

Like every mother's boy he loved and hated
smudging the future photograph she had
yet struggled within the frames of her eyes and then
froze for her, the noted naturalist –
her very affectionate and famous son.
But when most surely in her grasp, his smiles
darting and enfolding her, his words:
'Without my mother's help …' the dream occurred.

Dozens of flying things surrounded him
on a green terrace in the sun
and one by one
as if he caught caresses in his palm
he caught them all and snapped and wrung their necks
brittle as little sticks.

Then through the bald, unfeathered air
and coldly, as a man would walk
against a metal backdrop, he
bore down on her
and placed them in her wide maternal lap
and accurately said their names aloud:
woodpecker, sparrow, meadowlark, nuthatch.

❧ Paranoid

He loved himself too much. As a child was god.
Thunder stemmed from his whims,
flowers were his path.
Throughout those early days his mother was all love,
a warm projection of him
like a second heart.

In adolescence, dark and silent, he was perfect;
still godlike and like a god
cast the world out.
Crouching in his own torso as in a chapel
the stained glass of his blood
glowed in the light.

Remained a god. Each year he grew more holy
and more wholly himself.
The self spun
thinner and thinner like a moon forming
slowly from that other self
the dead sun.

Until he was alone, revolved in ether
light years from the world,
cold and remote.
Thinking he owned the heavens too, he circled,
wanly he turned and whirled
reflecting light.

❧ Typists

They, without message, having read
the running words on their machines,
know every letter as a stamp
cutting the stencils of their ears.
Deep in their hands, like pianists,
all longing gropes and moves, is trapped
behind the tensile gloves of skin.

Or, blind, sit with their faces locked
away from work. Their varied eyes
stiff as everlasting flowers.
While fingers on a different plane
perform the automatic act
as questions grope along the dark
and twisting corridors of brain.

Crowded together typists touch
softly as ducks and seem to sense
each other's anguish with the swift
sympathy of the deaf and dumb.

🐦 Elegy

This spring is all small horses and stars
but you have closed your pores to its bombardment,
shut yourself up with the night that flowed into you like ink.

When that black haemorrhage began
your doors opened as if to sunlight
and the darkness roared in like a tidal bore.
Now your least thought is the poor type on cheap newsprint.

What whiteness in you called to be cancelled, pulled
darkness from the two opposing poles
so that you dribble black when you speak
to the accompaniment of muffled drums?

You, white and sewn with scarlet once,
walked giddy with gold
your gilded name grew in our heads and shone
now black is the colour of our true love's name.

First we mourned you as if dead
and covered you with flowers
but when the blackness trickled on our hands
we stepped out of your deadly nightshade.

And if we cry now it is because your green tree
turned too rapidly into coal
and because we have seen our whole hearts
and known them black-edged as mourning envelopes.

And because the stars of this spring will not dazzle our eyes
nor the small white horses accept sugar
lightly with feathered lips from such pied palms.

ϰ Cullen

Cullen renounced his cradle at fifteen,
set the thing rocking with his vanishing foot
hoping the artifice would lessen the shock.
His feet were tender as puffballs on the stones.

He explored the schools first and didn't understand
the factory-made goods they stuffed in his mind
or why the gramophone voice always ran down
before it reached the chorus of its song.
Corridors led 'from' but never 'to',
stairs were merely an optical illusion,
in the damp basement where they hung their coats
he cried with anger and was called a coward.
He didn't understand why they were taught
life was good by faces that said it was not.
He discovered early 'the writing on the wall'
was dirty words scrawled in the shadowy hall.

Cullen wrote a note on his plate with the yolk of his egg
saying he hardly expected to come back,
and then, closing his textbooks quietly,
took his personal legs into the city.
Toured stores and saw the rats beneath the counters
(he visited the smartest shopping centres)
saw the worm's bald head rise in clerks' eyes
and metal lips spew out fantasies.
Heard the time clock's tune and the wage's pardon,
saw dust in the storeroom swimming towards the light
in the enormous empty store at night;
young heads fingering figures and floating freights
from hell to hell with no margin for mistakes.

Cullen bent his eye and paid a price
to sit on the mountain of seats like edelweiss –

watched the play pivot, discovered his escape
and with the final curtain went backstage;
found age and sorrow were an application,
beauty a mirage, fragrance fictionary,
the ball dress crumpled, sticky with grease and sweat.
He forgot to close the stage door as he went.

He ploughed the city, caught on a neon sign,
heard the noise of machines talking to pulp,
found the press treacherous as a mountain climb:
all upper case required an alpenstock.
Tried out the seasons then, found April cruel –
there had been no Eliot in his books at school –
discovered that stitch of knowledge on his own
remembering all the springs he had never known.
Summer grew foliage to hide the scar,
bore leaves that looked as light as tissue paper
leaves that weighed as heavy as a plate.
Fall played a flute and stuck it in his ear,
Christmas short-circuited and fired a tree
with lights and baubles; hid behind Christ; unseen
counted its presents on an adding-machine.

Cullen renounced the city, nor did he bother
to leave the door ajar for his return;
found his feet willing and strangely slipping like adders
away from the dreadful town.
Decided country, which he had never seen
was carillon greenness lying behind the eyes
and ringing the soft warm flesh behind the knees;
decided that country people were big and free.
Found himself lodgings with fishermen on a cliff,
slung his hammock from these beliefs and slept.

Morning caught his throat when he watched the men
return at dawn like silver-armoured Vikings
to women malleable as rising bread.
At last, the environment was to his liking.
Sea was his mirror and he saw himself
twisted as rope and fretted with the ripples;
concluded quietness would comb him out:
for once, the future managed to be simple.

He floated a day in stillness, felt the grass
grow in his arable body, felt the gulls
trace the tributaries of his heart and pass
over his river beds from feet to skull.
He settled with evening like a softening land
withdrew his chair from the sun the oil lamp made,
content to rest within his personal shade.
The women, gathering, tatted with their tongues
shrouds for their absent neighbours and the men
fired with lemon extract and bootlegged rum
suddenly grew immense.
No room could hold them – he was overrun,
trampled by giants, his grass was beaten down.
Nor could his hammock bear him, for it hung
limp from a single nail, salty as kelp.

Cullen evacuated overnight,
he knew no other region to explore;
discovered it was nineteen thirty-nine
and volunteered at once and went to war
wondering what on earth he was fighting for.
He knew there was a reason but couldn't find it
and marched to battle half an inch behind it.

Five

❧ Alphabetical

A curious concept – *afterwards*
bearing the phantom of *before* within it.
Old-fashioned novelists fell back
on *afterwards*
to conjure up the sexual act
or when referring to religious conversion:
'afterwards her life was entirely changed.'

A shadowy comparison always implicit.

*

Before is something else. I run with it.
Before the industrial revolution
before Christ, before man
before life on this earth.
Whizzing backwards to another state.
Infinity
the ultimate destination.

Before is prelapsarian.
When I still read with care
Woolf, Maeterlinck, and Pirandello
conjurors of
the world that lay in wait –
before the metal entered, altering
the chemical components of my blood …

*

Who would wish carefulness on anyone?
And yet to care is vital, so, to care
to fullness should be better still.
Yet carefulness is often merely caution
a loss of nerve, the doubter's fall-back position.

*

On good days I can doubt the very floor
I stand on, even doubt the ageing flesh –
my hand, or yours.
On bad days doubt is absent and I lock
solidly into matter. Staunchly in.

*

Even. An intensive. Useful word.
To emphasize the character of something or
to indicate the unexpected or
to stress the comparative.
Even is also steady, level, flat,
without a break. Or fair
Or
balanced, even.

*

My ancestors came from the Essex fens
where winds blew in from the sea
and chilled their bones and destroyed their lungs.
They died young.
Land like a cold plate.

Alberta – flat too if you looked eastward.
I preferred the foothills, rode up from the plains
on my cayuse into the mountains.
Closer to God.

*

God. There's a subject for a book or two.
As if there aren't enough of them already.
How strange that we imagine a bearded man.
The blame can't all be laid on Blake
who painted the Ancient of Days.

Christians and Jews supplicate God the Father.
Confucius and Buddha – male.

Allah is not.

In realms like this the human comprehension
is no better than a hammer
reducing everything to a nail.

*

How easy to believe humanity is
top banana on the evolutionary tree
Ha, ha!
Ignorance and ego are a pair!
If you read Rumi you will have to think again.
Read Rumi. Think again.

*

I, I, I, I, I say. I. I.
I think, I talk, I walk, I this, I that.
Ignorance is the root of it, how else
imagine so narrow a vertical slot
could let in Jupiter, the god of light?
And why – come to think of it – do we see the self
as single? More like a crowded room.

*

In astrology – to which
I pay lip service while unconvinced –
sun signs and planets rule,
not parents or heads of state.

Jupiter in my Aries is
the greater fortune, crown, and thunderbolt.

I love him most
as eagle.

The young Iranian
eating falafels looked like a bird of prey
and when I asked what he did, 'Sky dive' he said.
'I ride the currents. Need it like a drug.'
I dove all the livelong night that night
on currents of air.
Kissed the eagle, beak to beak.

*

Let us consider kissing. Nothing to do with love.
Or something. Sometimes.
But not as world-wide a custom as one might suppose.
That being so
I am curious to know
what, in those unkissing cultures,
they do with their lips?

*

Love. There's another word for you. All but perished.
A concept with an inadequate label. *Love* won't do.
As many kinds as the Inuit's words for snow.
What is it you feel for your mother?
For your dog?

I once was caught in its slipstream
and like dust
in a ray of sunlight
everything shone.

*

Growing up on the prairie we were hooligans.

Our eastern cousins thought we had long nails
and dressed in skins. Would that we had had!
Had.

Instead we were models of propriety: gloves and
stockings in midsummer.
None but my mother
thought it absurd.

Thirty years later travelling in New Guinea
the ladies of the administration
wore long white kid gloves to tea
a formality unheard of surely even in Court circles.

Racism or loneliness. A need to conjure
a remembered or invented past.
Dinner jackets in the jungle.

*

How define, fine tune, the line
between greed and need?

Ask a starving man.

You can argue, of course, that everyone is needy
Rilke's 'emptiness' not flung out of our arms.
Longing a lodger
for life.

Home from abroad
I saw my countrymen's faces
alight and shining
and leaning closer to hear some wonder or other –
heard them describe
like prisoners dreaming
steaks they had eaten with mushrooms
or Black Forest cake.

*

Or – 'a function word
to indicate an alternative' –
while giving us choices, narrows our options;
is
as reductionist as *I* is, O
eliminate it, take it away, we require
all the doors and windows open. Remove the roof
tile by virtual tile, take down the walls.
Paradise is merely an *or* away. Or is it?

*

For all its imperfections, it was perfect.
Nearly unending summer, windmills that turned
vegetable vanes, animals with pockets,
flowers to delight an embroiderer, talking birds.

Next question?

Paradise was what I called it.
They
called it Brazil.

*

Your questions are often laziness, my father said.
Learn to ask
only when you have tried and failed
to find answers.

He taught me independence early,
how to use a dictionary, an encyclopedia,
reference books of all kinds. Made me push
towards objectivity.

*

The Spanish say they check the dictionary
to see if it's correct.
A good attitude
to reference books in general, those
faceless authority figures in disguise.

*

The Alhambra with its honeycombings,
archways of stone lace,
reflection-pools to trap the light,
polychrome tiles, the elegant Kufic script ...
Ai! my heart breaks in Spanish.
Aiee!

*

Think about traps.
First about trapping light.
The spire on the steeple traps
the last light of the day.
A puddle traps the sky.

Now think of a child imagining leg-hold traps,
then growing up to set them.

The bone of mink or marten snapped, the wild
animal wild with pain gnawing its leg.
How understand the trapper's
heart, his head —
two of the many inhabitants in that crowded room.

*

Is understanding
part of consciousness?
But only accessible sometimes?

Alternating current, perhaps.

Or does the brain,
deliberate as a hand
turning a tap,
turn consciousness off
when the persona
fearing a flood
is no longer able to bear
so starry a totality
so vast a space?

The very me of me gone?

Who then?
Then what?

*

As a child I was wakened
taken from my tent
to look at the velvet
vastness of the night.

I had never seen my parents' eyes
so glistening,
such wonder on their faces
like the look of love
they gave me in the mornings.

Standing between them
barefoot on the prairie
I looked deeper and deeper in.

Eternity rushed past.

*

We set forth
on this long journey
sleeping.

How waken
when
we think we are awake?

Each least xx, xy
its mother's marvel
moving from school
to marriage
then to children —
and what more real
and wide awake than children?

So dynasties begin
and we their founders.

Surely
we could not do *this*
in our sleep.

*

Arithmetic bored me —
I thought it a tool for housewives —
but in my teens
the tidy
algebraic knot
the perfect puzzle
the code of x plus y
the beautiful clean
equilibrium of equations
fired me.
I was a sudden mathematician.

This love was purer
than my passion for pig Latin
and those difficult linguistic
'pigs' that followed.

Should I, instead, have been
a cipher clerk?

*

On the computer keyboard
Yes and No
hide behind Y and N.
A binary choice.

No equivalent
for de Bono's munificent *po* –
poetry, *possibility*, the prefix *poly* –
a chance
to see around corners
or enter
the scale between extremes.
To fly – perhaps.

Sooner rather than later
we also learn
that lower case l is not the number one.
Upper case O is never zero.

Zero is zero.

*

I have circled zero
over and over
in love with the aperture
where the face of light
might appear.

With Euclid's compass
I draw beautiful circles.
I trace man-hole covers, ride Ferris wheels,
wear rings on my fingers –
all are zero.
A port-hole awaiting that luminous face.

How visualize nothingness –
rare gift from Arabia –
absence of all magnitude?

And – afterwards?

How anticipate
afterwards?

Six

❧ The Apple

Look, look, he took me straight
to the snake's eye
to the striped flower
shielding its peppery root.

I said, I shall never go back.

At harvest he took me around and about.
The ground
was apple red and round.
The trees bare.
One apple only hung like a heart in air.

Together bite by bite
we ate,
mouths opposite.
Bit clean through core and all to meet:
through sweet juice met.

I said, I shall never go back.

But someone let an angel down
on a thin string.
It was a rangy paper thing
with one wing torn,
born of a child.

Now, now, we come and go, we come and go,
feverish where that harvest grew.

✹ The Figures

These equal lines refused their triangle –
the two-dimensional figure they were given.
Varied their groupings, always one was single.
Potential equal angles were unproven.
Met, forming points at ac and bc
but a and b refused. The two lines rose
perilous uprights, wavering, uneasy,
balancing delicately at ninety degrees.
So formed a figure wanting to be square
whose outline finding itself incomplete
might draw d to it from the empty air
to consummate its quadrilateral need.
And it was as it dreamed, and the square was,
with all its lines and all its angles equal.
Fit diagram for any textbook this,
sharp black on white, exact, symmetrical.

❧ Autumn

Whoever has no house now will never have one.
Whoever is alone will stay alone
Will sit, read, write long letters through the evening
And wander on the boulevards, up and down …

'Autumn Day', RAINER MARIA RILKE

Its stain is everywhere.
The sharpening air
of late afternoon
is now the colour of tea.
Once-glycerined green leaves
burned by a summer sun
are brittle and ochre.
Night enters day like a thief.
And children fear that the beautiful daylight has gone.
Whoever has no house now will never have one.

It is the best and the worst time.
Around a fire, everyone laughing,
brocaded curtains drawn,
nowhere – anywhere – is more safe than here.
The whole world is a cup
one could hold in one's hand like a stone
warmed by that same summer sun.
But the dead or the near dead
are now all knucklebone.
Whoever is alone will stay alone.

Nothing to do. Nothing to really do.
Toast and tea are nothing.
Kettle boils dry.
Shut the night out or let it in,
it is a cat on the wrong side of the door
whichever side it is on. A black thing
with its implacable face.
To avoid it you
will tell yourself you are something,
will sit, read, write long letters through the evening.

Even though there is bounty, a full harvest
that sharp sweetness in the tea-stained air
is reserved for those who have made a straw
fine as a hair to suck it through –
fine as a golden hair.
Wearing a smile or a frown
God's face is always there.
It is up to you
if you take your wintry restlessness into the town
and wander on the boulevards, up and down.

❧ Unable to Hate or Love

In sight of land, everything came at him sharp and bright –
gulls suddener and a higher light on the wave.
New seeing made him a stranger to himself
and now, no longer one of the boys, he was quite alone
and lost in the larger body he had grown
during the sea trip; found himself shy
even with friends and nervous about the soil.

When the carrier came to dock he stood on deck
close-pressed among the rest. From the waiting bus
there to despatch him to a camp, he was
identical with the others – a khaki boy
released to freedom, returning from the East.
And though he had longed for freedom, found it hard
to visualize the walk along the street
or conversing with a girl
or the girl's speech.

It was almost as if there were figures behind his eyes
that he couldn't completely see around or through:
as if in front of him there were others who
partially blocked his view, who might even speak
gibberish or cry if he opened his mouth.

He wished, for the moment, he needn't go ashore
into this unknown city of friends. Already
the mayor had welcomed them by radio,
the sirens that hooted and screamed had made him a fool,
the people lining the docks were weeping for him
and everywhere hankies and flags fluttered but he
came from an unnamed country.

Three years he had dreamed this moment and how, running
he would tear with his smile the texture of this air;
he had dreamed that peace could instantly replace war.
But now he was home and about to land and he feared
the too-big spaces and the too-blue skies
and knew, at last, that most of his dreams were lies
and himself a prisoner still behind his face,
unable to be free in any place;
to hate the enemy as they wished him to
or love his countrymen as he would like to do.

❧ The Castle

It is the stress that holds the structure up.
Birds in its turrets tilt it not at all.
Balance is inner, centred in the keep.

Marble and timber crumble as we sleep.
Centuries of creeper cannot sustain a wall.
It is the stress that holds the structure up.

Lovers in spirals, turning in the deep
well of their rapture, dizzyingly recall
balance is inner, centred in the keep.

Patients, post-crisis, feel the fever drop.
The pendulum begins its swing from ill to well.
It is the stress that holds the structure up.

Whoever – dreaming – dances a tightrope
knows where is balance, just before the fall!
Balance is inner, centred in the keep.

Insomnia, pain and trouble have a stop
definitive, sudden, at the terminal.
It was the stress that held the structure up.
But balance is inner, centred in the keep.

❧ Love's Pavilion

Though they go mad they shall be sane,
Though they sink through the sea they shall rise again;
Though lovers be lost love shall not;
And death shall have no dominion.

    'And Death Shall Have No Dominion', DYLAN THOMAS

Tell me the truth. How does it end?
Who will untangle their matted hair?
Shine in the dark hole of their sleep?
Though they rattle the stones in their broken brains,
in their thicket of words who will find a way,
discover a path through unmapped terrain?
When will the unpretentious air
fall like rain on the ache of their skin?
What is the price they pay for pain?

Though they go mad they shall be sane.

What is the hope for those who drown?
Pickled in brine? Stripped to the bone?
Who will they meet in deep sea lanes?
Or, when they find themselves alone,
too far up or too far down
beyond the reach of hell or heaven
how will they speak who have no tongue?
Who will they be when their bones are gone?
Bodiless, are they anyone?

Though they sink through the sea they shall rise again.

And what of the heart like an empty cup;
heart like a drum; red blood – white?
How can they twin when their love has gone?
How can they live when their love has died?
When the reins to their chariot have been cut?
What of the plot and counterplot
families devise to keep apart
Romeo from Juliet?
And what of the lovers of Camelot?

Though lovers be lost love shall not.

Love shall not. O, love shall not.
Engrave it in stone. Carve it in rock.
This is the subtext of all art,
the wind in the wings of the Paraclete.
With the Lord of the Dance we shall form a ring
and there in love's pavilion
hand in hand we shall say Amen
and we shall dance and we shall sing
with Love, with Love for companion.

And death shall have no dominion.

❧ Cry Ararat!

I

In the dream the mountain near
but without sound.
A dream through binoculars
seen sharp and clear:
the leaves moving, turning
in a far wind
no ear can hear.

First soft in the distance,
blue in blue air
then sharpening, quickening
taking on green.
Swiftly the fingers
seek accurate focus
(the bird
has vanished so often
before the sharp lens
could deliver it)
then as if from the sea
the mountain appears
emerging new-washed
growing maples and firs.
The faraway, here.

Do not reach to touch it
or labour to hear.
Return to your hand
the sense of the hand;
return to your ear
the sense of the ear.
Remember the statue,

that space in the air
which with nothing to hold
what the minute is giving
is through each point
where its marble touches air.

Then will each leaf and flower
each bird and animal
become as perfect as
the thing its name evoked
when busy as a child
the world stopped at the Word
and Flowers more real than flowers
grew vivid and immense;
and Birds more beautiful
and Leaves more intricate
flew, blew and quilted all
the quick landscape.

So flies and blows the dream
embracing like a sea
all that in it swims
when dreaming, you desire
and ask for nothing more
than stillness to receive
the I-am animal,
the We-are leaf and flower,
the distant mountain near.

II

So flies and blows the dream that haunts us when we wake
to the unreality of bright day:
the far thing almost sensed by the still skin

and then the focus lost, the mountain gone.
This is the loss that haunts our daylight hours
leaving us parched at nightfall
blowing like last year's leaves
sibilant on blossoming trees
and thirsty for the dream of the mountain
more real than any event:
more real than strangers passing on the street
in a city's architecture white as bone
or the immediate companion.

But sometimes there is one
raw with the dream of flying:
'I, a bird,
landed that very instant
and complete –
as if I had drawn a circle in my flight
and filled its shape –
find air a perfect fit.
But this my grief,
that with the next tentative lift
of my indescribable wings
the ceiling looms
heavy as a tomb.

'Must my most exquisite and private dream
remain unleavened?
Must this flipped and spinning coin that sun
could gild and make miraculous become
so swiftly pitiful?
The vision of the flight it imitates
burns brightly in my head as if a star
rushed down to touch me where I stub against
what must forever be my underground.'

III

These are the dreams that haunt us,
these the fears.
Will the grey weather wake us,
toss us twice in the terrible night to tell us
the flight is cancelled
and the mountain lost?

O, then cry Ararat!

The dove believed
in her sweet wings and in the rising peak
with such a washed and easy innocence
that she found rest on land for the sole of her foot
and, silver, circled back,
a green twig in her beak.

The leaves that make the tree by day,
the green twig the dove saw fit
to lift across a world of water
break in a wave about our feet.
The bird in the thicket with his whistle
the crystal lizard in the grass
the star and shell
tassel and bell
of wild flowers blowing where we pass,
this flora-fauna flotsam, pick and touch,
requires the focus of the total I.

A single leaf can block a mountainside;
all Ararat be conjured by a leaf.

🗡 Visitants

Each afternoon at four bird after bird
soars in and lands in the branches of the oaks.
They stamp about like policemen. Thick boots
almost visible in the lacy leaves.
No, those are birds, not boots, clumsy, heavy
leaf-rustlers who tear at twigs and rend
the living bone of the tortured trees and pelt
the lawn below — thup, thup, thup — with acorns.
They give no cry, no coo — a flock of mutes
overhead, deaf mutes perhaps, unhearing
the flail and storm they make stuffing, stuffing
their gullets and sleek bellies with salad fruits.

Through binoculars they are beautiful,
the prettiest pigeons — every feather
each neat little head, white collar, banded tail.
But voracious, gang-despoilers of the treetops
they shake and thrash about in, tiny eyes
riveted upon acorns ah they are gone in a whoosh
wooden rackety twirling noisemakers
and we left hungry in this wingless hush.

❧ Out Here: Flowering

I have not been a tree long enough yet.

JONATHAN GRIFFIN

Such stern weather. Metallic. When I was a human child
my surrogate mother smiled like that –
frostily from stone eyes – no heart in it –
a withering blasted cold
that coated me with ice – I, a small tree glistening in a field
of glassy snow – shot
beautifully through with rainbows and somehow – absolute.
But spoiled. Utterly spoiled.

No wonder the blossoming has been slow,
the springs like flares, the crowding flowers
a surfeit of whipped cream. How many years have I stood sere
brown and unseasonable in the subliming air?
But now the melt has begun and the weather pours
over me in a pelt of a petalled snow.

✒ Funeral Mass

In his blackest suit
the father carries the coffin

It is light as a box of Kleenex
He carries it in one hand

It is white and gold
A jewel box

Their baby is in it

In the unconscionable weather
the father sweats and weeps

The mother leans
on the arms of two women friends

By the sacred light of the church
they are pale as gristle

The priests talk Latin
change their elaborate clothes

their mitres, copes
their stoles embroidered by nuns

Impervious to grief
their sole intention

is the intricate ritual
of returning a soul to God

this sinless homunculus
this tiny seed

❧ The Hidden Components

In his palace
the ravaged king
while simple in exile and rags
his falsely dishonoured queen

Naked now in the jungle
safe in a leafy nest
their radiant son and daughter
wards of a giant bird

I see the king's black face
the rigid line of his jaw
He is on stage centre
blind to the hidden components

The queen is harder to see
She is almost transparent   Who
can look through such a window?
The view is a single flower
For some it is white linen

The king is a charred ruin
The queen looks forward and back
Royal castaways, the children
understand the language of birds

More than the sum of their parts
they cannot see one another
the king in his palace the queen
the children safe in the jungle

Cannot foresee that the king
crazed with grief at his loss
wandering deep in the jungle
will discover the royal children

Cannot foresee that the children
a diminutive queen and king
will recognize their father
remember their royal blood

Cannot foresee that the bird
homing into the jungle
will bear on her feathered back
the falsely dishonoured queen

The hidden components await
the possible perfect moment
the invisible conjuror
the triangulation of stars

Meanwhile the king is a ruin
the exiled queen is a window
the children safe in the jungle
converse in the language of birds.

❧ The Glass Air

I dreamed my most extraordinary darling
gangling, come to share
my hot and prairie childhood

the first day loosed the mare from her picket
and rode her bareback
over the little foothills towards the mountains.

And on the second, striding from his tent,
twisted a noose of butcher's string.
Ingenious to my eyes the knots he tied.

The third bright day he laid the slack noose over
the gopher's burrow,
unhurried by the chase,

and lolled a full week, lazy, in the sun
until the head popped, sleek, enquiring.
The noose pulled tight around its throat.

Then the small fur lashed, lit out, hurling
about only to turn
tame silk in his palm

as privy harness, tangled from his pocket
with leash of string
slipped simply on.

But the toy beast and the long rein and the paid-out lengths
of our youth snapped
as the creature jibbed and bit

and the bright blood ran out, the bright blood trickled over,
slowed, grew dark
lay sticky on our skins.

And we two, dots upon that endless plain, Leviathan became
and filled and broke
the glass air like twin figures, vast, in stone.

❧ The Metal and the Flower

Intractable between them grows
a garden of barbed wire and roses.
Burning briars like flames devour
their too innocent attire.
Dare they meet, the blackened wire
tears the intervening air.

Trespassers have wandered through
texture of flesh and petals.
Dogs like arrows moved along
pathways that their noses knew.
While the two who laid it out
find the metal and the flower
fatal underfoot.

Black and white at midnight glows
this garden of barbed wire and roses.
Doused with darkness roses burn
coolly as a rainy moon;
beneath a rainy moon or none
silver the sheath on barb and thorn.

Change the garden, scale and plan;
wall it, make it annual.
There the briary flower grew.
There the brambled wire ran.
While they sleep the garden grows,
deepest wish annuls the will:
perfect still the wire and rose.

✺ Emergence

Come before rain;
rise like a dark blue whale
in the pale blue taffeta sea;
lie like a bar in the eyes where the sky should be.
Come before rain.

❧ Stories of Snow

Those in the vegetable rain retain
an area behind their sprouting eyes
held soft and rounded with the dream of snow
precious and reminiscent as those globes –
souvenir of some never nether land –
which hold their snowstorms circular, complete,
high in a tall and teakwood cabinet.

In countries where the leaves are large as hands
where flowers protrude their fleshy chins
and call their colours
an imaginary snowstorm sometimes falls
among the lilies.
And in the early morning one will waken
to think the glowing linen of his pillow
a northern drift, will find himself mistaken
and lie back weeping.
And there the story shifts from head to head,
of how, in Holland, from their feather beds
hunters arise and part the flakes and go
forth to the frozen lakes in search of swans –
the snow light falling white along their guns,
their breath in plumes.
While tethered in the wind like sleeping gulls
ice boats await the raising of their wings
to skim the electric ice at such a speed
they leap jet strips of naked water,
and how these flying, sailing hunters feel
air in their mouths as terrible as ether.
And on the story runs that even drinks
in that white landscape dare to be no colour;
how, flasked and water clear, the liquor slips
silver against the hunters' moving hips.
And of the swan in death these dreamers tell
of its last flight and how it falls, a plummet,

pierced by the freezing bullet
and how three feathers, loosened by the shot,
descend like snow upon it.
While hunters plunge their fingers in its down
deep as a drift, and dive their hands
up to the neck of the wrist
in that warm metamorphosis of snow
as gentle as the sort that woodsmen know
who, lost in the white circle, fall at last
and dream their way to death.

And stories of this kind are often told
in countries where great flowers bar the roads
with reds and blues which seal the route to snow –
as if, in telling, raconteurs unlock
the colour with its complement and go
through to the area behind the eyes
where silent, unrefractive whiteness lies.

❧ Old Man

Brought to earth – the runner with souvenirs.
Slowed to a standstill in a northern garden
he remembers the lazy houseboat at Kashmir,
tulips on the roofs of the public buildings,
the caravan in Germany,
girl in a trance
and the pony-cart he drove on the roads of France.

Now in his green-legged trousers and here where
he had never wished to be, in this new, this north
land with a foreign people he cannot know
he walks the wild bewildering woods alone
wearing a sweater
found a decade ago
high up among the gentians near the snow.

Read classics as a boy. At fifty threw
the blue and golden volumes from his room
in a hotel in Venice one clear noon.
Changed to detective tales of death bypassed
and certain comics –
Batman, Superman
which prove the last shall surely be the first.

Always he had loved the flowers and now for his eyes
camas lilies – Mary-blue – and gorse,
its sweetness on the air by the water; flowers,
a picnic of them – fritillary, Indian's purse –
better when picked
held in his ancient hand
than growing from a strange and foreign earth.

But now, war ending, exiled among winds
and too-familiar servants, he desires
Europe and yesterday – and the flowers pale
before his paling eyes and the vivid grass
fades to a wash.
He hates this pallid place
and dreams a bright green future in the past.

❧ The Bands and the Beautiful Children

Band makes a tunnel of the open street
at first, hearing it;
seeing it, band becomes
high; brasses ascending on the strings of sun
build their own auditorium of light,
windows from cornets
and a dome of drums.

And always attendant on bands, the beautiful children,
white with running and innocence;
and the arthritic old
who, patient behind their windows
are no longer split by the quick yellow of imagination
or carried beyond their angular limits of distance.

But the children move
in the trembling building of sound,
sure as a choir
until band breaks and scatters,
crumbles about them and is made of men
tired and grumbling
on the straggling grass.

And the children, lost, lost,
in an open space,
remember the certainty of the anchored home
and cry on the unknown edge of their own city
their lips stiff from an imaginary trumpet.

❧ Leather Jacket

One day the King laid hold on one of the peacocks
and gave orders that he should be sewn up in a leather jacket.

That peacock a prisoner
that many-eyed bird
blind.

Enclosed in a huge leather purse.
Locked in darkness.
All its pupils sealed
its tiny brain sealed
its light and fluttering heart
heavy as a plum.

Its life vegetable.
That beautiful colourful bird
a root vegetable.

Cry, cry for the peacock
hidden in heavy leather
sewn up in heavy leather
in the garden

among flowers
and flowering trees
near streams
and flowering fountains
among cicadas
and singing birds.

The peacock sees nothing
smells nothing
hears nothing at all

remembers nothing
but a terrible yearning
a hurt beyond bearing
an almost memory
of a fan of feathers
a growing garden

and sunshine falling
as light as pollen.

✹ Lily on the Patio

It's like a slender person in a pot
as tall as I am in my heels, a presence
perfumed, parasolled, imperious.
Dispassionate. Neuter. Mute.

A budding Beanstalk – but no Jack am I
nor Jill, to climb its spiky leaves to heaven.
And where the sun shines through it who can tell
its colour. Is it green chartreuse? Or yellow?

Swings like a yacht at anchor in some sweet
and imperceptible breeze,
some silken rearrangement of the air
– sleeves of kimonos loose –

to waft its inner essence on us where
in our gross human flesh we stupefy
while silently – a bare brown foot away –
its open-mouthed enamelled trumpets bray.

Silence is where it leads. Its phantom gift –
sheer voicelessness. Those swinging scented shafts
beamed from its lighthouse and oblivious
of noisy all of us

are like neutrinos touching us without our knowing.
Doing who knows what
as they pass through us?
Answer: *Who* knows what.

❧ Picking Daffodils

They have spilled their slippery juices over me
let fall saliva from their long green stems
Their viscous threads of water swing into my house
remind me of the waters of your mouth

✖ The Gift

'Dried huckleberries,' you said.
'Cram them into your mouth by the handful.'

Like dried bees – not quite stinging.
Rough and tart.
Chewy as a mouthful of springs.

My saliva releases
their ten small bony nutlets.

❧ Cook's Mountains

By naming them he made them.
They were there
before he came
but they were not the same.
It was his gaze
that glazed each one.
He saw
the Glass House Mountains in his glass.
They shone.

And they shine still.
We saw them as we drove –
sudden, surrealist, conical
they rose
out of the rain forest.
The driver said,
'Those are the Glass House Mountains up ahead.'

And instantly they altered to become
the sum of shape and name.
Two strangenesses united into one
more strange than either.
Neither of us now
remembers how they looked before they broke
the light to fragments as the driver spoke.

Like mounds of mica,
hive-shaped hothouses,
mountains of mirror glimmering
they form
in diamond panes behind the tree ferns of
the dark imagination,
burn and shake
the lovely light of Queensland like a bell
reflecting Cook upon a deck
his tongue
silvered with paradox and metaphor.

Seven

❧ Conchita Knows Who Who Is

Quien sabe, Señora? Quien sabe?
    Conchita speaks.
Who broke the plate, Conchita?
Quien sabe, Señora?
What day of the week?
Who knows?
What time of day?
Quien sabe? Quien sabe, Señora?
    Boredom. Despair. Evasion.
    Shades of unknowing.
Where is the key?
Conchita, whose shoes are these?
Quien sabe, Señora? Quien sabe.
Who knows? Who knows.

    Who knows.
    A statement of fact.
    Of faith.
    WHO knows.
    Who knows who is this WHO?
    Conchita knows.
    Conchita knows WHO knows who broke the plate,
    what day, what hour, who stands beside the gate
    and where the key, and whose the shoes …
    Conchita knows who WHO is,
    one vast WHO
    in whom all questions are resolved
    all answers hiding.

Quien sabe, Señora. Quien sabe.
    Indulgent. Wise.
    Don't worry *your* head about it, child.
    WHO knows.

℣ Portrait of Marina

Far out the sea has never moved. It is
Prussian forever, rough as teaselled wool
some antique skipper worked into a frame
to bear his lost four-master.
                          Where it hangs
now in a sunny parlour, none recalls
how all his stitches, interspersed with oaths
had made his one pale spinster daughter grow
transparent with migraines – and how his call
fretted her more than waves.
                          Her name
Marina, for his youthful wish –
boomed at the font of that small salty church
where sailors lurched like drunkards, would, he felt
make her a water woman, rich with bells.
To her, the name Marina simply meant
he held his furious needle for her thin
fingers to thread again with more blue wool
to sew the ocean of his memory.
Now, where the picture hangs, a dimity
young inland housewife with inherited
clocks under bells and ostrich eggs on shelves
pours amber tea in small rice china cups
and reconstructs
how great-great-grandpappa at ninety-three
his fingers knotted with arthritis, his
old eyes grown agaty with cataracts
became as docile as a child again –
that fearful salty man –
and sat, wrapped round in faded paisley shawls
gently embroidering.
While Aunt Marina in grey worsted, warped
without a smack of salt, came to his call
the sole survivor of his last shipwreck.

*

Slightly offshore, it glints. Each wave is capped
with broken mirrors. Like Marina's head
the glinting of these waves.
She walked forever antlered with migraines
her pain forever putting forth new shoots
until her strange unlovely head became
a kind of candelabra – delicate –
where all her tears were perilously hung
and caught the light as waves that catch the sun.
The salt upon the panes, the grains of sand
that crunched beneath her heel
her father's voice, 'Marina!' – all these broke
her trembling edifice. The needle shook
like ice between her fingers.
In her head
too many mirrors dizzied her and broke.

*

But where the wave breaks, where it rises green
turns into gelatine, becomes a glass
simply for seeing stones through, runs across
the coloured shells and pebbles of the shore
and makes an aspic of them
then sucks back
in foam and undertow –
this aspect of the sea
Marina never knew.

For her the sea was Father's Fearful Sea
harsh with sea serpents
winds and drowning men.
For her it held no spiral of a shell
for her descent to dreams,
it held no bells.
And where it moved in shallows it was more
imminently a danger, more alive
than where it lay offshore full fathom five.

⭐ Star-Gazer

The very stars are justified.
The galaxy
italicized.

I have proofread
and proofread
the beautiful script.

There are no
errors.

❧ Brazilian Fazenda

That day all the slaves were freed
their manacles, anklets
left on the window ledge to rust in the moist air

and all the coffee ripened
like beads on a bush or balls of fire
as merry as Christmas

and the cows all calved and the calves all lived
such a moo.

On the wide veranda where birds in cages
sang among the bell flowers
I in a bridal hammock
white and tasselled
whistled

and bits fell out of the sky near Nossa Senhora
who had walked all the way in bare feet from Bahia

and the chapel was lit by a child's
fistful of marigolds on the red velvet altar
thrown like a golden ball.

Oh, let me come back on a day
when nothing extraordinary happens
so I can stare
at the sugar-white pillars
and black lace grills
of this pink house.

After Rain

The snails have made a garden of green lace:
broderie anglaise from the cabbages,
Chantilly from the choux-fleurs, tiny veils –
I see already that I lift the blind
upon a woman's wardrobe of the mind.

Such female whimsy floats about me like
a kind of tulle, a flimsy mesh,
while feet in gumboots pace the rectangles –
garden abstracted, geometry awash –
an unknown theorem argued in green ink,
dropped in the bath.
Euclid in glorious chlorophyll, half drunk.

I none too sober slipping in the mud
where rigged with guys of rain
the clothes-reel gauche
as the rangy skeleton of some
gaunt delicate spidery mute
is pitched as if
listening;
while hung from one thin rib
a silver web –
its infant, skeletal, diminutive,
now sagged with sequins, pulled ellipsoid,
glistening.

I suffer shame in all these images.
The garden is primeval, Giovanni
in soggy denim squelches by my hub,
over his ruin
shakes a doleful head.
But he so beautiful and diademed,
his long Italian hands so wrung with rain
I find his ache exists beyond my rim
and almost weep to see a broken man
made subject to my whim.

O choir him, birds, and let him come to rest
within this beauty as one rests in love,
till pears upon the bough
encrusted with
small snails as pale as pearls
hang golden in
a heart that knows tears are a part of love.

And choir me too to keep my heart a size
larger than seeing, unseduced by each
bright glimpse of beauty striking like a bell,
so that the whole may toll,
its meaning shine
clear of the myriad images that still –
do what I will – encumber its pure line.

✈ Cross

He has leaned for hours against the veranda railing
gazing the darkened garden out of mind
while she with battened hatches rides out the wind
that will blow for a year or a day, there is no telling.

As to why they are cross she barely remembers now.
That they *are* cross, she is certain. They hardly speak.
Feel cold and hurt and stony. For a week
have without understanding behaved so.

And will continue so to behave for neither
can come to that undemanded act of love –
kiss the sleeping princess or sleep with the frog –
and break the spell which holds them each from the other.

Or if one ventures towards it, the other, shy,
dissembles, regrets too late the dissimulation
and sits, hands slack, heart tiny, the hard solution
having again passed by.

Silly the pair of them. Yet they make me weep.
Two on a desert island, back to back
who, while the alien world howls round them black
go their own ways, fall emptily off to sleep.

❧ Giovanni and the Indians

They call to pass the time with Giovanni
and speak an English none can understand
as Giovanni trims the weeping willow,
his ladder teetering in the yellow leaves.

They make him teeter even when he's steady;
their tatters blow and catch him through the trees;
those scraps of colour flutter against stucco
and flash like foreign birds;

and eyes look out at eyes till Giovanni's
are lowered swiftly – one among them is
perhaps the Evil Eye. The weather veers.
Pale leaves flap wetly on the metal trees.

                    *

Bare winter is pure glass. Past panes of air
he peers but sees no colour flicking raw
behind the little twigs; no movement shakes
the sunlight on the berries, no branch cracks

till quakes of spring unsettle them. Their flocks
emerge, they sprinkle paths with petals.
Now Giovanni pauses, stares and shrugs
hiding behind a golden blind of wattle.

                    *

One on a cycle, like a ragged sail
that luffs and sags, comes tacking up the hill.
Does Giovanni smile as he darts off, low
over the handlebars of his spinning wheel?

And one, his turban folded like a jug,
and frocked, walks brittle on his blanco'd legs –
a bantam cockerel. Giovanni looks
and laughs and laughs and lurches in great loops

and stoops to bend above a bed and gather
hyacinths, tulips, waterblue and yellow;
passes his offering through the rainy willow
nodding, 'Good fellow,' smiling, 'much good fellow.'

❧ On Educating the Natives

They who can from palm leaves and from grasses
weave baskets of so intricate a beauty
and simply as a girl combing her hair,
are taught in a square room by a square woman
to cross-stitch on checked gingham.

✎ Exile

There will only be yesterday, only the fading land,
The boats on the shore and tamarisks in the sand
Where the beautiful faces wait, and the faithful friends.
They will people your mind. You will never touch their hands.

   'Imagine the South', GEORGE WOODCOCK

Tomorrow a change of lens or soft-focus filter
will alter the past. Its edges will smudge and blur,
its embroideries and its subtleties disappear.
It will be generic, unparticular
unlike today which is bright as a name brand, clear
and familiar as the palm of your hand.
And though you may squint and shade your eyes and peer
back through time, mists will obscure the scene.
Whatever you long for has been left behind.
There will only be yesterday, only the fading land.

And memory, trickster figure, will let you down –
a fiction writer offering alternative versions
of what you had once imagined written in stone:
the immutable facts of your life. But now you question
which of them are true, and truth itself
that once appeared an end to be sought and found
becomes elusive, seems to assume disguises;
is finally and, heartbreakingly, diminished
to a dim discoloured shot of low tide and
the boats on the shore and tamarisks in the sand.

And as for the people you loved, even their names
will escape you. Did you not mean what you said
when you said, I will love you forever? You did.
Though it's hard to remember when now you can barely recall
the lift of the chin or the quizzical tilt of the head
that filled you with wonder, or how you counted the seconds
that felt like hours, for a glimpse ... but you know the rest –
any more than your eye can recapture the angle of light
as it fell on the valleys and hills of those distant lands
where the beautiful faces wait, and the faithful friends.

They will wait and wait forever –
become like figures from dreams, or phantom limbs.
How beautiful they are, how blossoming
in your imagination. Trees in spring.
And the pain of their absence, harder to bear than death,
is with you wherever you go – a secret wound
that aches in the night, awakens you from sleep
and makes you a child again, a lonely child.
And so they will haunt you, those half-remembered friends.
They will people your mind. You will never touch their hands.

Domestic Poem for a Summer Afternoon

The yellow garden-chair is newly webbed.
There, Arthur, full-length, reads of 'Toronto the Golden',
dozes, nods, lets fall his magazine.
From a golden book I read of Arthur, the King,
and Taliessen, the King's poet. I dream of the crown.
Was it jewelled with rubies, emeralds, stones the colour of his eyes?

The ducks are within arm's reach as usual
at this time in the afternoon — two mallards, webbed
feet tucked out of sight, they float
in unreflecting emerald grass. They doze.
Might be decoys, these wild water birds
unmoving as wood.

It is hot. Siesta still.
Not hot enough for Brazil but I think of Brazil
and the small yellow bird that flew in and perched
on the toe of Arthur's crossed-over foot,
puffed out its feathers, settled down for the night;
and the hummingbird, ruby-throated, a glowing coal
with the noise of a jet
that landed cool and light on the crown of his head.

We are settled down for the afternoon,
with whispering sprinklers and whirring jets.
We are so motionless we might be decoys
placed here by higher hunters who watch from their blind.
Arthur asleep has the face of a boy.
Like blue obsidian the drake's head glints.
His mate and I are brown in feather and skin
and above us the midsummer sun, crown of the sky,
shines indiscriminate down on duck and man.

❧ Presences

There they were as our guests, accepted and accepting.
So we moved, and they, in a formal pattern,
Along the empty alley, into the box circle,
To look down into the drained pool.

  'Burnt Norton', T.S. ELIOT

Extraordinary presences, the sunlight seeming
to light them from within, tall alabaster
amphoras with flames inside them
motionless within the grove, their shadows
like chlorophyll, like leaves, like water
slipping from a silver jug, reflecting
grasses, the long pliant stalks of willows.
And when they turned to us, their brightness spilled
over our skin and hair and, like a blessing,
there they were as our guests, accepted and accepting.

Only our golden selves went forth to greet them
that part of us which receiving blows
feels neither pain nor grief, the part that senses
joy in a higher register and moves
through a country of continuous light
shed by the one god, by the sun god, Aten –
moves as Nefertiti and her daughters
moved through their city of continuous light
in the pharaonic kingdom of Aknaten.
So we moved, and they, in a formal pattern.

Our feet barely touched the earth, and memory
erased at birth, but gradually reassembling
coalesced and formed a whole, as single birds
gathering for migration form a flock.
And some new incandescence in our heads
led us from the shadows to the sparkle
of Aten-light where we at last remembered
the arc of our lives, the distant stars we came from
and walked – O joy, O very miracle! –
along the empty alley, into the box circle.

And so to the maze with its forking paths which seen
from above, entire, was like a map –
or like a rose unfolding, a yellow rose,
opening in the unreflecting air –
the green of its leaves
the Garden before the fall,
every atom accurately aligned,
and there we walked in youthful innocence
until we came at last – new-born, royal –
to look down into the drained pool.

❧ The Answer

For whom do you live? Can it be yourself?
For whom then? Not for this unlovely world,
Not for the rotting waters of mischance,
Nor for the tall, eventual catafalque.

'The Vow', ROBERT GRAVES

Tell me every detail of your day –
when do you wake and sleep, what eat and drink?
How spend the interval from dawn to dark –
what do you work at, read, what do you think?
Whom do you love and how much? – Measure it
and answer me, or leastwise, answer half.
These are not idle questions, they provide
the spindle around which new-spinning wool
winds as it dreams its future warp and woof.
For whom do you live? Can it be yourself?

No. Your answers prove it – they are tinged
with another pigment, glow with light
from a strange sun, *contre-jour*, backlit –
a light that would have taxed all Monet's skills
and, fading, left him knowing he had failed.
Your answers, though transparent, issue veiled,
hermetic, deeply hidden; you speak in code.
A huge enigma hides in your replies.
Not live for the self – first love, unparalleled?
For whom then? 'Not for this unlovely world,

'world we have made unlovely, world we have used,
as if it were ours to tamper with, ours to destroy
and so we have destroyed it, like a child
taking his father's watch apart, or worse, a fly –
removing its prismed, fragile wings.
Destroyed it not for myrrh or frankincense,
but gold, O Midas. We have sacked for gold.
Nor do I live for what it could have been
had we been otherwise. Not for providence,
not for the rotting waters of mischance,

'but love, only for love, the love that is
so focused on its object that I die
utterly, a candle in the sun,
a drop of water in the sea.
I do not live for heaven's promises
in fear of purgatory or hell's deadlock
but for that beam of love which clothes us in
ephemeral garment's coronation cloth –
not wealth, not jewels, not sovereignty, not silk
nor for the tall, eventual catafalque.'

❧ Intraocular Lens Model 103G

This lens I look through is as clear as glass.
It shows me all I saw before was false.

If what *was* true is true no longer, how
now can I know the false true from true true?

✴ Invisible Presences Fill the Air

I hear the clap of their folding wings
like doors banging or wooden shutters.
They land and settle – giant birds
on the epaulettes of snowed-on statues.

On grass one drops its greenest feather.
On the head of a blond boy, a yellow.
The red feather on my heart falls plumb.
Do not ask about the whitest feather.

I feel them breathing on my cheek.
They are great horses dreaming of flight.
They crowd against me. Are outsize.
Smell of sweet grass. Smell of hay.

When in my heart their hooves strike flint
a fire rages through my blood.
I want water. I want wool.
I want the fruits of citrus trees.

Their eyes flash me such mysteries
that I am famished, am ill-clad.
Dressed in the rags of my party clothes
I gather their hairs for a little suit.

O who can name me their secret names?
Anael, opener of gates.
Phorlakh, Nisroc, Heiglot,
Zlar.

❧ War Lord in the Early Evening

Suitable for a gentleman with medals
to choose for pleasure
and his beneficent care
the long-stemmed roses wilting in the summer weather.

Fitting for a man in his position
to succour them with water
at his side
admiring, dressed in muslin, his small daughter.

He saw the picture clearly. It was charming:
the battered war lord
in the early evening
among the roses, gentle and disarming.

The way he sent the servants for the hoses
they thought a fire was raging
in the garden.
Meanwhile the roses and the light were fading.

Six choppy lengths of tubing were assembled.
Bind them, the general stormed
from six make one.
Was this philosophy? It wasn't plumbing.

How bind six hoses of assorted sizes
all minus fixtures?
Though his servants shrugged
they dropped to a man on their knees and bound their fingers

tightly around the joints and five small fountains
gushed at specific places
on the lawn
and cooled five straining servants' sweating faces.

Pitiful the little thread of water
that trickle, that distil.
The darkness hid
a general toying with a broken water pistol.

Hid from his daughter, frail organza issue
of his now failing loin
the battle done:
so much militia routed in the man.

Sic transit gloria mundi. I would rather
a different finish.
It was devilish
that the devil denied him that one innocent wish.

ꔷ The Selves

Every other day I am an invalid.
Lie back among the pillows and white sheets
lackadaisical O lackadaisical.
Brush my hair out like a silver fan.
Allow myself to be wheeled into the sun.
Calves'-foot jelly, a mid-morning glass of port,
these I accept and rare azaleas in pots.

The nurses humour me. They call me 'dear'.
I am pilled and pillowed into another sphere
and there my illness rules us like a queen,
is absolute monarch, wears a giddy crown
and I, its humble servant at all times, am its least
serf on occasion and excluded from the feast.

Every other *other* day I am as fit
as planets circling.
I brush my hair into a golden sun,
strike roses from a bush,
rare plants in pots
blossom within the green of my eyes, I am
enviable O I am enviable.

Somewhere in between the two, a third
wishes to speak, cannot make itself heard,
stands unmoving, mute, invisible,
a bolt of lightning in its naked hand.

❧ Journey

Never resist the going train of the dream
risen and steaming on hard tracks
through Breughel landscape
or troubled slum.

The houses and the faces fabricate
heart's drop to terror and eyes' flight to madness;
cling, madam, to the blunt caboose like a streamer
or prod the engine.

Oh, do not lag behind syringe of whistle
douching your ears; on spongy fingers
number the revs. per min.
They are your tempo.

You may be boxcar baggage or begonia,
porter with epaulettes and moon for navel;
the way is watercolour to the station,
the stop is limbo.

❧ Index of Titles

❧ Acknowledgements

My warmest thanks to Eric Ormsby, poet and editor, who has chosen the poems for this selection and written the introductory essay; to Théa Gray, Arlene Lampert, Constance Rooke and Rosemary Sullivan whose critical comments over the years have done me nothing but good. And last but not least, to my husband Arthur Irwin, who is invisibly present in my books as in my life.

Acknowledgments are due also to The Hawthorne Society of Arts and Letters for the first publication of 'Alphabetical', to *Border Crossings* for 'Cosmologies', and to Poppy Press and Alexander Lavdovsky for a deluxe boxed edition of both poems. 'A Grain of Sand' was written at the request of Derek Holman for his oratorio, *The Invisible Reality*, performed at Roy Thomson Hall in 2000. Finally, thanks to the Porcupine's Quill for the poems reprinted from *The Hidden Room*.

❧ About the Author

P.K. Page has written some of the best poems published in Canada for over five decades. In addition to winning the Governor General's award for poetry in 1957, she was appointed a Companion of the Order of Canada in 1999. She is the author of more than a dozen books, which include ten volumes of poetry, a novel, selected short stories, three books for children, and a memoir entitled *Brazilian Journal* based on her extended stay in Brazil with her late husband Arthur Irwin who served as the Canadian Ambassador to Brazil from 1957 to 1959. A two-volume edition of her collected poems, *The Hidden Room*, was published in 1997.

She also paints under the name P.K. Irwin. She has mounted one-woman shows in Mexico and Canada, and has been exhibited in various group shows. Her work is represented in the permanent collections of the National Gallery of Canada, the Art Gallery of Ontario and the Victoria Art Gallery, among others.

P.K. Page was born in England and brought up on the Canadian prairies. She has lived in the Maritimes and Montreal. After years abroad in Australia, Brazil and Mexico, she now makes her permanent home in Victoria, British Columbia.